To Jim Neice

You made some excellent contributions to our sessions. Thanks for your observations. Best of success in the future.

Best Regards,

John H. Neice

Modern Persuasion Strategies:
The Hidden Advantage in Selling

MODERN PERSUASION STRATEGIES: THE HIDDEN ADVANTAGE IN SELLING

Donald J. Moine
and
John H. Herd

Prentice-Hall, Inc.   Englewood Cliffs, New Jersey

Prentice-Hall International, Inc., *London*
Prentice-Hall of Australia, Pty. Ltd., *Sydney*
Prentice-Hall Canada, Inc., *Toronto*
Prentice-Hall of India Private Ltd., *New Delhi*
Prentice-Hall of Japan, Inc., *Tokyo*
Prentice-Hall of Southeast Asia Pte. Ltd., *Singapore*
Whitehall Books, Ltd., Wellington, *New Zealand*
Editora Prentice-Hall do Brasil Ltda., *Rio de Janeiro*

©1984 *by*

PRENTICE-HALL, INC.

Englewood Cliffs, N.J.

Sixth Printing . . . . . November 1988

Library of Congress Cataloging in Publication Data

Herd, John H.
  Modern persuasion strategies.

  Includes index.
  1. Selling—Psychological aspects.   I. Moine, Donald J.
II. Title.
HF5438.8.P75H47 1984   658.8′5   84-11552

ISBN 0-13-596099-1

Printed in the United States of America

DEDICATION

For Katherine, Debby, Thomas, and Claudia

For Tony, Molly, and Linda

Foreword

I am not your typical sales executive. At least I don't think I am. I learned at the age of ten as a milkman's helper the importance of being customer-driven. This "customer first" creed stuck with me as iceman's helper, coalman, paperboy, newspaper station manager, tool and die apprentice, tool buyer for one of the Big Three auto makers, and as founder of my own successful insurance agency, in which I also functioned as top personal producer. These experiences, followed by 18 years of hard work in multi-national operations with my present employer, led to my current assignment as Vice President of Sales for one of the world's largest tooling companies with a 600-person direct sales force serving the free world. In the process, I have once again become a serious student of selling— its methods and its magic. The process is totally fascinating to me.

As a buyer and purchasing agent I met a great many salespeople. A few left an indelible impression on my mind because of their professional skills, dedication, and their ability to build a trust relationship. They had what today is called "the unique factor" or what I like to call "sales magic." Why? Because I believed I was in good hands when dealing with them. I could trust them. They usually met or exceeded my expectations. After making the transition from operations to sales I asked myself, "How can we deliberately build a sales force having that unique factor?"

Our search began by reviewing a number of nationally famous sales courses. They were of high quality. We were invited to test them with small segments of our group. Our people's acceptance and the results did not deliver what we were looking for, and we continued our search. In the process I learned of an interesting experiment conducted by the industrial division of a major appliance manufacturer. They assigned their new sales representatives to understudy their best sales performers by working side by side with them in the field. Their hope was that the special skills of the senior salespersons would by osmosis transfer to the newcomers. It did not work that way most of the time. The junior sales people picked up primarily what they could have learned in any good sales course. *What happened to the magic? What happened to that unique factor?*

During this same time period I received a call from John Herd, a business acquaintance of long standing. He asked for a half-hour of my time to bounce an idea off me. Since we had worked together successfully on two projects before, I was receptive to his suggestion. It turned into a most interesting meeting because he described what we had been searching for without knowing it existed! Only he did not call it sales magic; he called it sales logic. "Did your people report," he asked, "that the logical approach of probing doesn't work as well as it once did?" "Yes," I said. "Would your salespeople agree that selling is much more than a rational process, that it is primarily an emotional process?" "Yes," I said, "it must be, considering the sometimes illogical decisions rational people seem to make." "Would you be willing to run a series of pilot programs with our people to test their reaction and acceptance?" "Yes."

Today, just six months after our first pilot program, 400 domestic and Canadian salespersons, as well as the European general managers have gone through a customized sales program. Our sales have increased dramatically. We have maintained our marketshare with significantly fewer people...in a fiercely competitive price market. Our orders are back to prerecessionary levels. Certainly some part of this turnaround is the result of the improved economic climate. But by itself it does not explain the magnitude of the comeback.

I believe it is the special training we got from John Herd and Don Moine, described in this book, that made the big difference. Our salespeople not only immediately accepted this new information, but were able to go out in the field and use it with success. They began to read people in a new way. They became better observers and listeners. Their sales awareness increased. They targeted on the customer's needs, feelings, and goals. They were able to get some customers out of mental ruts. They have greater insights into their own personalities and those of the people they call on. They have a better perspective of the drama that occurs in a sales interview and know how to guide it in a positive way for all concerned. Now they truly have "Sales Magic" and what is more *they know they have it!*

THE VALERON CORPORATION

William J. Herman
Vice President
Worldwide Sales

February 20, 1984

Introduction

Usually, an introduction is for the purpose of telling you what benefits will come to you from the book you are holding in your hand, what problems is it unearthing, and how it is solving them. This true dialogue, changed somewhat in the interest of brevity, may well make the point intended.

A short time ago I received a telephone call from a ranking sales executive of one of the best known information processing companies in the land. He said, "We have the best sales training available. We train our people in consultative and non-manipulative selling, in features benefits selling, in gate selling, in reverse question techniques to let the customer do most of the talking, in probing questions and decision-making strategies, and in behavioral style. Tell me, how come these things do not seem to work as well as they once did?"

"Because," I heard myself saying, "those techniques do not train your people in how to read people so that they can respond to them emotionally. All influencing, all persuasion, all selling is primarily emotional. What you are teaching them is rational, and that is fine. What sells is emotional, or what we call sales logic. We have high-tech clients whose requests for proposals run in the hundreds of millions sometimes. They will tell you that reading and treating the customer correctly is their single biggest challenge. When everything is the same, it is the salesperson who makes the difference. We buy from people who are like ourselves. Once sales professionals understand and accept this natural law and operate within it, there is no stopping them."

"How do you get them to do this?" he continued.

"First they learn how to build trust and rapport quickly, often within minutes, regardless of the generation gap or differences in income, social or educational background, or sex. Would that be important to some of your younger people?"

"It is a major concern of ours," he said.

"They learn, when face to face, how the prospect thinks and makes buying decisions about your product or service and then make their presentation accordingly."

"Go on."

"They listen to how the prospects express themselves, which enables them to speak the prospects' favorite language, or what we call information bias. More?"

"If you will."

"Suppose someone has trouble paying attention to you. We train you to sound interesting by changing how you talk in a specific way, which is designed to appeal to that specific listener. That is important when talking to groups."

"Right."

"Best of all, we introduce your people to entirely new ways of defusing even the toughest objections. We use mental judo and a technique called refocusing your listener's mind set. It alters his or her perspective of what is important in making a particular decision and helps to arrive at better choices for everyone."

"Is this not a little sophisticated?"

"People who have gone through the experience tell us it is even more basic than Selling 101, yet more advanced than current methods. It is completely state-of-the-art."

You might now ask, "Is this for me?" It is for you if you want to influence customers, clients, patients, subordinates, superiors, or constituents. It is for you if you want to learn and practice what the greatest communicators, sales greats, leaders, and executives do unwittingly and could never explain before. It is for you if you want to surpass yourself when interacting with people and having fun at the same time. It is for you if you are interested in not being pushy or dreary when you're with people. It is for you if you are interested in *Modern Persuasion.*

WHAT IS MODERN PERSUASION?

Modern Persuasion is the ability to see, to hear, and to feel what other people miss, and to respond to the prospect in interesting ways. It is completely customer-focused. Derived from neuro-linguistic programming, semantics, systems, cybernetics, synectics, negotiation, and cold reading, Modern Persuasion is an ethical method of influencing that proves astonishingly effective in reading another person's informational prejudices, in building trust and rapport rapidly, in leading him or her unobtrusively, and in guiding his or her emotions to a successful outcome. Like an infrared scope, it lets you see situations that seem totally dark and inexplicable to others.

Modern Persuasion is based on our observation and research with more than 100 of the country's sales luminaries, who themselves cannot consciously describe how they perform their own sales magic. After studying them in action, reviewing their tapes, and testing the newfound insights in the field, we were able to help increase sales in various companies from as little as 17 percent to as much as 232 percent in a span of one year.

HOW THIS BOOK CAME TO BE WRITTEN

Donald Moine was working his way through college as a salesman when he learned of the ground-breaking research of two communication scientists, Richard Bandler and John Grinder, who pioneered the discipline of neuro-linguistic programming (NLP) at the University of California. He sensed that NLP strategies might help explain extraordinary sales success and began his research utilizing and testing some of the powerful techniques himself. By adding to the available knowledge, he steadily increased his sales success ratio in the field. With the publication of his findings on Modern Persuasion, several national corporations, including Singer, Hughes Aircraft, and Control Data, and a major intelligence arm of the U.S. government called on him for consulting services. *Psychology Today* magazine published his findings in the lead article in its August 1982 issue.

John Herd is an internationally recognized authority on sales and management productivity. The recipient of numerous awards and honors, John has been Salesman of the Year for two major corporations. In many years his income from personal selling matched that of top corporate presidents. A consultant to Fortune 500 companies and president of the Achievement Center, John saw early on the vast number of potential applications of NLP to sales and management. He realized, however, that it had to be supplemented with other disciplines, especially in the realm of refocusing techniques to help direct prospects to choosing better options, thus making Modern Persuasion practical to sales and business professionals.

Donald Moine and John Herd have now worked with nearly 100 of the world's greatest salespeople, who handle everything from glamorous high-tech products to mundane staples and commodities, who engage in high-volume "pocket money" deals to seven-figure transactions. They have recognized and documented one common bond among these great producers: Modern Persuasion Strategies. The new forms of influence shared with you in this book are bringing success to organizations and individuals alike. They will work for anyone who is willing to put them into practice.

Donald J. Moine
John H. Herd

Contents

PART IV TECHNIQUES FROM SALES SUPERSTARS

PART I
BUILDING TRUST AND RAPPORT

1

The Science of Building Trust and Rapport

Lou Barth, a specialty food salesman in New York and Philadelphia, is a genius at pacing. His customers run the spectrum from wholesalers of ethnic foods to chic purveyors of gourmet specialties.

Many consider him a legend, for Lou has a knack of adapting himself to his customers, so that his visit becomes the high point of their day. "There is only one of you, Lou," they say. "You are the greatest." They love him because he is like them. He is one of them.

To the grandmotherly German widow now in charge of her late husband's food emporium, Lou is the warm, affable, and considerate son who remembers to send her a get well card and chocolates.

To the owner of the prestigious Charles of Madison Avenue, Lou is the polished, sophisticated businessman, impeccably attired, who looks and acts like his senior partner.

To the food wholesaler's street-smart staff, Lou is the quick-witted traveler, who knows just one more joke, one more hip expression, and one more expressive gesture than they do. He is their hero.

Everyone feels better for having Lou around. He communicates that he is like them. Yet Lou is no phony. He is at all times honest and true to his person. Lou has great people sense. He is an expert in reading his customers and is aware of subtle changes in their faces, their voices, their eyes, and their bearing.

When calling on them, he shows those facets of himself that are easiest for them to relate to.

In the language of Modern Persuasion, Lou "paces" the customer. Research reveals that *pacing* is a sophisticated form of matching or mirroring key aspects of another person's behavioral preferences. It is used almost continually by top salespeople—those sales luminaries who sometimes produce five or ten times more than other hard-working salespeople. They earn that much because, in addition to having outstanding products and service, they build trust and rapport quickly and deeply with prospects, often in minutes.

Without trust and rapport, a salesperson is like the farmer who tries to sow on untilled soil. Most of the seed will be wasted.

Trust lowers interpersonal tension and makes the prospect more comfortable with you. The prospect opens up more and freely reveals information regarding personal needs, wants, objectives, and goals. Without trust it is difficult and sometimes impossible to sell even the best product. On Alan Funt's "Candid Camera" show, a lack of trust stops people from buying a $20 bill for $3.

In discovering the difference between top and average salespeople, Modern Persuasion research shows, for example, that overeager salespeople move into their presentations too quickly and lose orders as a consequence. Like the inexperienced batter, they swing at every ball that comes their way. In their eagerness to make a sale, they end up working a lot harder and longer. They encounter more stalls and objections, largely because the important elements of rapport and trust are missing and are not sufficiently nurtured during the sale.

FORTY-THREE NEW CLIENTS IN ONE DAY

Sandy Shinn went through college under a premed program and then decided against becoming a doctor. She joined the laboratory services group of an international pharmaceutical corporation, where her mission was to persuade doctors to let her company process their lab samples.

For Sandy, it was a difficult road to travel, especially since her company was neither the cheapest nor the fastest. Her prospects saw no reason to change and were in fact tied to their current labs because of computer billing arrangements. But you have to know Sandy. She is down-to-earth, really likes people, and shows it. Even though her immediate prospects were far from bright, she decided to do three things:

- She would regularly visit her prospects with some new information designed to be of interest to them.
- She worked on building rapport, never showed her frustration or disappointment, and would comment, "We both have something to look forward to, because we will be doing business one of these days."
- She built trust by letting it be known that she had completed premed, could speak their language, understood their problems, and was always an interested listener.

Her first goal was to be the number two source to their present laboratories. Dramatically, in a wholly unexpected way, her rapport building has paid off. "Sixty Minutes" did a story on kickbacks to doctors by certain laboratories, one of which served the doctors in Sandy's area. Although there were competitive labs, 43 doctors switched their allegiance to Sandy and her company.

The many months of unfaltering goodwill and rapport paid off, and Sandy became the first woman ever to be national sales leader in her group for two years running.

BUILDING TRUST AND RAPPORT THROUGH PACING

You are pacing the prospect effectively to the degree that you and the prospect seem to be in agreement or alignment. You are pacing when the prospect gets the feeling that you and he or she think alike and look at problems in similar ways. When this happens, the prospect identifies with you and finds it easy and natural to agree with you. You seem like emotional twins. Pacing works because like attracts like.

Pacing signals to the prospect, "I understand you. I accept you. I am like you." By pacing, you step into the prospect's world of reality, his or her private thoughts and emotions. You can accomplish this with word or behavior and without the prospect's conscious awareness.

HOW PACING WORKS

The healthy-minded individual is interesting because of the many facets of his or her personality. Every time you are with another person, you have the choice about what facets you want to display. Modern Persuasion research indicates that less successful salespeople tend to show only one or two aspects of themselves, no matter whom they are with or what the situation demands. This is why a rigid or inflexible person generally will not make it to the top in the highly demanding world of sales and management.

Sales superstars like Lou Barth intuitively present themselves in ways most like their customers without compromising their integrity in any way. They are merely being flexible and adaptable in showing parts of their true personalities. They know they can always find some common ground between themselves and their prospects.

One great benefit of pacing is that, when it is properly done, your prospect finds it virtually impossible to disagree with you. To do otherwise would require the prospect to disagree with himself or herself, a notion that most people will not entertain.

Pacing statements are verbal photographs. Like a film image, they offer no new information yet fascinate the viewer. They are undeniably true. When presented in sequence they lead to a series of minor agreements called yes-sets and ultimately lead to a major agreement or sales contract. Pacing statements stroke the prospect because they focus attention on the prospect and his or her world.

Once trust and rapport are established, the leading or guiding can begin. It is the leading statements that contain the persuasive messages. The most beautiful leading statements, however, will be ineffective unless trust in the relationship is built first.

Pacing statements can range from the mundane to the arcane and cover emotional or factual material.

Here is an observational pacing statement made by a top Mercedes Benz salesman to a prospect who is in his showroom: "I notice you first looked at the white convertible and then at the coupe and then at the turbo diesel, and then you went back to the convertible."

He does not say, "Can I help you?" which may trigger a negative response. Instead, he gives a description of what the prospect had in fact done. Since it is undeniably true, it is impossible to disagree with. As the salesman speaks, the prospect nods slightly. The salesman establishes minor agreement early and sets the stage for further agreement.

The governor of a western state begins his address,...The unemployment rate is 9.8 percent, and here in our state it is 10.1 percent....

Then, following up with additional figures, even his adversaries find themselves entering into initial agreement with him and scarcely notice his smooth transition into the leading statements that tell his intended message. Later he says, "I can only talk from my own limited experience."

Nobody can disagree with that pacing statement, because it is true for all of us. Yet this modest admission helps him get the audience on his side.

While it is important to begin using pacing statements when meeting a prospect, its use is not limited to the early part of the interview. Pacing can be used throughout the sale, but especially at the beginning and when handling objections. Each time you pace, you weave another strand into the fabric of interpersonal relations and make it stronger. This is why pacing sets up closer ties. We can learn a lesson here from great statesmen, who know how to return to undeniably truthful facts, even trivial facts, when faced with strong or disagreeable confrontation.

Pacing offers a powerful new dimension in Modern Persuasion and requires the pacer to become a keen and more caring observer of others. It does not require memorizing formulas about what to do, but rather concentrates attention where it belongs—on the prospect and his world.

CONTROLLING THE PAST, THE PRESENT, AND THE FUTURE

Modern Persuasion research shows that the more thoroughly a person has been paced, the easier it is to lead or influence him or her.

Comedian Mort Sahl tells us that Lyndon B. Johnson had a legendary reputation as a peacemaker in the Senate. When facing a tough situation requiring all of his skills, he'd begin by pacing the opponent:

Johnson: "Jim, you and I go back a long ways and we usually have been able to come to terms." (Pacing the past.)

Senator: "That's right." (Minor agreement.)

Johnson: "Now, I know we are both agreed on the importance of point A. Isn't that right?" (Pacing previous agreement in the past.)

Senator: "True." (Minor agreement.)

Johnson: "And, I believe you and I are not far apart on point B. So, let's work on that and see where we can agree." (Pacing the present.)

Senator: "OK." (Minor agreement.)

Johnson: "After that, point C shouldn't be so hard." (Pacing the future.)

With the minor agreement established, the emotional logic was hard to break. While what Johnson said was certainly general, it was said with such feeling that it generated much conviction and momentum. This method of pacing the past, present, and future works effectively for many "natural-born" salespeople.

How can you use pacing? Think of a difficult prospect and list all of the possible characteristics you can match in that person. Then list experiences you can talk about in an undeniably truthful manner. Now practice pacing that person. Your experience will convince you that these methods are indeed the heart of trust-building.

CONTROLLING THE EMOTIONAL CLIMATE

Do you recall the last time you were down, depressed, or under the weather? Imagine someone coming up to you and saying, "Cheer up, man. It's a great day! Today is the first day of the rest of your life! I'm feeling great, and you can, too! Come on! Let's have some of that positive mental attitude!"

Would that cheer you up? Most people would find it irritating and insensitive. Your friend failed to align himself with you or to show that you shared common ground. He didn't pace your mood. Rather than pacing and then leading you, he wanted to force you directly into feeling better. While this direct "hit-them-over-the-head" approach can sometimes work, it is usually an abysmal failure.

There is probably more misunderstanding about enthusiasm and positive mental attitude in sales and management than any other subject. Both characteristics are wonderful to possess and experience. They are, however, easily overused. They are no substitute for getting in step with people's feelings.

The compulsively cheerful salesperson is a museum relic and has long outlived his or her usefulness. Today's sales professional has to be a problem solver, a relationship expert, and a complete businessperson.

Hale and hearty salespeople are notably successful with hale and hearty prospects. When calling on a business that is struggling to stay alive, however, the grinning hyena approach does not establish much rapport. While there is much to be said for being enthusiastic, there is even more to be said for being flexible. Modern Persuasion research shows that one-dimensional salespeople and managers, no matter what their dimension is, do not reach the highest levels of success.

When your prospect or coworker seems sad or depressed, respect his or her mood. Speak the language of his or her feelings. Top salespeople teach us that an individual in a bad mood can actually be one of the easiest to sell. Once he or she feels you are in step and understand, you can begin leading. Suppose you are having a bad day and someone were to comment, "You know, I'm not myself today. I don't know why, so I'm just taking each day as it comes. But I can still find a few things I enjoy doing. Like talking to a friend or going out for a walk. Do you think you might want to walk out with me to pick up a little snack?"

Here your mood is matched or paced, and then you are gently led to another feeling state. You would probably feel much safer with that person than with the one who tries to force you into a good mood.

We encounter people with all sorts of moods in daily life—some sad, some happy, some thoughtful, some carefree. In addition, one's own mood can change from hour to hour. This is where the importance of flexibility becomes apparent. Pace the mood of your prospects and coworkers and you will find trust and rapport relatively easy to establish. People will feel closer to you. Obviously, we are not advocating becoming depressed when you are with a depressed person. All that is necessary is to match the mood temporarily. Feel free to show more animation and good cheer after a few minutes, but use mood pacing as a touchstone of commonality you can return to.

Suppose a tight-lipped, unemotional corporate controller interested in a new car is greeted by an outgoing, backslapping, extroverted salesperson. Would they be likely to hit it off? It is doubtful. In polite terms, they may say, "I don't relate to someone like that." Assume that the controller wants a model that is in stock and available at a fair price. Would the controller buy from that salesperson? Perhaps, but without trust and rapport the odds are not good.

In sales and management you face many days when you cannot predict the moods of the people you will encounter. Remember that no matter where you want to lead your prospect or coworker, the best place to start is where he or she is at. While it sounds simple, it does take practice to develop this skill.

You can practice on the best trainers in the world—your prospects, customers, and fellow workers. It is safe to do and very respectable. They will not know what you are doing but will be aware that they feel better when you are around. That is the beauty of pacing.

PACING BODY LANGUAGE

The evening before keynoting a national sales conference recently, I was introduced to a top producer in the corporation. This salesman shook my hand for a solid five minutes, and I in turn paced the exact grip and tempo of his handshake. I also paced his mood and vocal characteristics. Even though we discussed nothing of great consequence, this man later relayed to the senior vice-president that Dr. Moine impressed him as a most knowledgeable and genuine consultant. It was the pacing that built the trust. Even though we were from different parts of the country and he was my senior by 25 years, we quickly established rapport through pacing.

We communicate with one another through messages. Albert Mehrabian and other well-known communications researchers have clearly established that body language—how we look and carry ourselves—accounts for 55 percent of the total impact of the messages we send. The significance of this finding is that body language has greater impact on others than the content of what we say or how we say it.

When our words and our body language contradict each other, others will believe the body language. Suppose you are interviewing a candidate for a key position and you ask, "Can you tell me something about yourself?" Now your candidate shuffles his feet, he flushes slightly, beads of sweat break out on his forehead, and he looks down and stammers, "Well, I'm self-confident." Will you believe his words or his body language?

In studies of inner-city youth gangs, two major leadership styles were identified. One is the idea man, who is continually a step ahead of the rest of the gang. He's the talker, the mover, the shaker. The other is the stable leader. He intuitively paces the other gang members' body language, speech, and behavior. This type of gang leader is a keen listener and observer of others and is seen as being understanding and reliable. The members have faith in him.

HANDLING THE CHALLENGE OF NEGATIVE BODY LANGUAGE

Since body language is so important in the communication process, it is the subject of numerous books. While excellent research is available, most authors of popular books seem unfamiliar with it. Or, where research is cited, they sometimes draw simplistic and misleading conclusions from it. Perhaps most misunderstood is what is called negative body language.

Suppose you are talking with a customer whose arms are crossed. According to the authors, this posture means the individual is being defensive or is rejecting you. They suggest that you terminate the sales call or reschedule it for a better day.

If you followed this advice, you would walk out of many promising and profitable situations.

Crossed arms can signal defensiveness or many other emotions, depending on the individual. Modern Persuasion research has shown that some people cross their arms simply because it feels comfortable, others because it keeps the stomach warm, and still others to nurse a tennis elbow. By itself it is a fallacy to assume that one particular posture always has one meaning.

While body language does not lend itself to simplistic interpretations, it does have great value to the salesperson who can quickly put it to use with his or her pacing techniques. This is done through assuming the posture and gestures of the other person. In doing so, you will find it easier to relate to him or her. You'll feel more akin to that person, and he or she will feel more comfortable with you. You will, in a sense, be in that person's shoes. Most importantly, the other person will trust you and feel you understand and accept him or her.

It is unnecessary to imitate the other person's body language. In our research we find that top salespeople establish similarities in postures and gestures with customers and clients, but do not mirror them. In this way, the customer is not consciously aware of what you do, but experiences a positive effect about you at the subconscious level. You may be surprised to see people smiling at you for no apparent reason at all.

Some people are surprised to learn that research reveals that top sales producers even pace the negative body language of their listeners. By temporarily adopting the customer's negative body language, they initially establish agreement on a nonverbal level. Simultaneously, they are pacing on several verbal levels and pace mood. After developing trust and rapport they lead the customer from a negative to a positive posture. Usually the customer changes with them. What happens if it doesn't work on the first or second attempt? They repeat the sequence until it succeeds. Even when the customer returns to negative posture, they pace again. That reestablishes rapport, and they then lead the customer out of the negative body language. The untrained observer misses the entire scene; it all seems like pure magic.

Do you ever sit in a restaurant and try to guess which couples are really in love and which may be headed for a breakup? Your guesses may be surprisingly accurate. Couples in love intuitively pace each other's body language: they lean in the same direction, move in synchrony, and even tend to eat and drink in harmony with each other. Couples with problems or heading for the divorce court are out of harmony in their body language, their opinions, and their beliefs.

Likewise, top sales producers intuitively build intimacy in sales situations using the same type of body language pacing. When persuading or selling next time, avail yourself of this technique and experience how well it works for you and your listener.

PACING THE CUSTOMER'S BREATHING

American business is currently adopting management techniques from the Japanese. Yet there is one we are almost completely ignoring. Business and quality circle meetings in Japan start with all members breathing in unison—in together, out together, in together. This establishes a climate of agreement and harmony. It is not done for exercise, but because it makes good business sense. Studies show that as these meetings get under way, the executives in attendance bypass small matters and concentrate on the important issues.

In similar fashion, marriage and family counseling specialists now have disagreeing couples begin their sessions by putting their arms around each other and breathing in unison—in together, out together. This builds harmony and establishes a climate that does not nourish trivial differences.

To establish an unconscious affinity with others, breathe as they breathe. Notice that you become more relaxed as you do so and that it is completely undetectable on the conscious level. All the other person knows is that he or she feels closer to you. We experiment with pacing breathing even on sophisticated psychologists and find that none of them detect it.

Many top sales producers naturally match their customers' breathing without knowing it. When we point out what they are doing, they deny it. Only after viewing videotapes of themselves with customers do they recognize consciously the power they possess. Obviously, none has ever shared this method with his or her sales trainees. After seeing it in action, these sellers immediately accept its utility.

Observe couples in love and notice how they tend to breathe in unison. It does take some observational skills to pick up breathing pacing. Watch the chest expand and contract, watch the shoulders rise on inhalation and drop on exhalation, or watch the stomach for breathing rhythm.

By making a conscious effort to make the pacing techniques a part of you, you will find that people like to relate to you more than ever before.

2

How to Use
Your Voice
to Best Advantage

We trust people who are like we are. Studies of business executives show that we even tend to hire people who are like we are. It may not be fair, but the first people fired in business are often the people least like those in power. The psychologist William H. Sheldon, in classic studies done in the 1940s and 1950s, found that we are likely to marry people whose body styles are similar to our own. That is, tall skinny people tend to marry tall skinny people, and shorter, heavier people tend to marry their matches. While there are obviously many exceptions, the statistics have held that likes do attract likes.

Since the human personality is multifaceted, we have a choice at each moment in time about which facet we wish to show to any individual. We can pace or match mood characteristics, body language, and even breathing. Another way we express our individuality and judge other people is through our speech styles and vocal characteristics. Knowing how to control and project one's voice is becoming increasingly important as more and more sales and management work is being done over the phone. Products that for many years were sold face-to-face are now being sold successfully over the phone. For example, Zond, the largest wind turbine company in the United States, is currently selling $200,000 wind turbine generators with a telemarketing sales force!

Even the best sales presentation or the finest sales script will lose much of its effectiveness if it is not delivered in a way your prospect understands or can relate to. Much of the power of what we say is in how we say it. Albert Mehrabian and other highly respected researchers found that 38 percent of the power of what we say is not in the words themselves, but in how we say them.

Have you ever dealt with someone who talked so slowly you couldn't remember what he or she started out to say? Have you found yourself getting impatient with these slower-than-molasses speakers?

As uncomfortable as you were, the other person might have been even more ill at ease. To him or her, you might have sounded like a 33 rpm record spinning at 45.

The key to pacing is to remember that each of us thinks he or she is normal. We serve as our own reference standard and judge others against ourselves. The slow talker feels he or she talks at a normal rate. If you speak at his or her rate, you will be perceived as normal. You will be better understood and will be felt to be more trustworthy.

If you slow down your speech when speaking to a slow talker, chances are slight that it will be consciously noticed. However, if you continue talking at your faster rate, the odds are high that the difference will be detected and that there will be some resistance. It is much safer, and more respectful, to adjust your speech rate to more closely approximate that of your listener.

How do fast talkers make you feel? How do you think they feel with you? A fast talker might perceive you as being in a time warp or a little slow upstairs. The fast talker, according to his or her own internal reference standard, feels he or she is talking at a normal rate. When you speed up your vocal delivery a bit, he or she will perceive that you are more normal or at least less different. If you had the opportunity to see the brothers and sisters of this fast talker, the chances are that they each speak quickly, too. Therefore, when you speak somewhat more quickly, you tap into this built-in trust dynamic. You subconsciously fire off associations and feelings that have been built in over many years of intimate interactions with others.

Be sensitive to your customers', prospects', and coworkers' rates of speech. Increase your ability to speak at another person's rate of speech. Get into the habit of purposefully matching speech rate. Your experience will convince you that this can increase interpersonal rapport and decrease tension.

While speech rate is a useful lever for gaining trust, don't attribute more meaning to it than is there. For example, don't assume that a slow talker is suffering from a mental or intellectual deficit. In some parts of the country, slow speech is simply a part of the culture. A fast talker is not perceived as sharp or smart, but simply as different, and is automatically somewhat distrusted. There are individuals and families in all parts of the country who speak slowly. You don't have to psychologize or try to guess the meaning of this. Just pace the given speech rate and enjoy the benefits of increased trust and rapport.

Managers and sales supervisors can use their knowledge of speech rate pacing to good advantage in training their subordinates. Go on calls with your people and note when they pace speech rate and when they ignore it. Our experience shows that the best people have much more sensitivity, awareness, and flexibility in this area, much of it intuitive. We can now use the findings of Modern Persuasion to reach this important ability in others.

We can take a lesson here from J. R. Ewing of Ewing Oil in the television drama "Dallas." The writers and producers wanted J. R. to be seen as untrustworthy. They made him a fast talker in a world of slower talkers. The gut-level response from those around him and from most viewers is immediate and just as programmed: Don't trust this man. You don't want your salespeople or employees to inadvertently trigger this response in your customers. Teach them to pace speech rate and all of the other aspects of behavior.

SCREAMS AND WHISPERS

We were working with some commodity salespeople at a large national brokerage house. During our needs assessment, it became apparent that many of the salespeople had supervisors or role models who taught them to scream at clients over the phone.

...Mr. Prospect, buy gold! Buy silver! The Russians just shot down a Korean passenger plane with a U.S. congressman on board! It's chaos! There could be war! Everyone is running scared! The smart money is all going into gold and silver! *All* the money will be going into gold and silver! No one will want paper money! Come on, let me get you in with the big boys! I want to make you rich! I want to make you a fortune! Let's Go!!!!...

We found that the ploy worked to some degree during a crisis, but soon lost its impact from overuse. To sophisticated investors who had heard it all before, the ploy was seen for what it was. Designed to create a sense of urgency, it instead created distrust.

We do trust people we perceive as being like we are, and this extends also to speech volume. People who speak softly are very aware of screamers and whisperers. They consider their own speech volume normal and intuitively trust others who speak at their level.

Those who speak more loudly may not trust or be inspired by the soft talker. Research has found that louder people tend to judge whisperers as insecure, self-conscious, nervous, weak, and wimpy. While these quick judgments are often not justified and may later be corrected with much work, they are guiding impressions nonetheless. As is said in advertising, "You never get a second chance to make a first impression."

Pacing speech volume is an outstanding opportunity to develop subliminal ties with your customers, prospects, and coworkers. The only safeguard we recommend is to avoid screaming *at* a screamer. This can be a battle cry signaling the start of a bloody war. Instead, scream (or raise your voice) *with* the screamer at some outside object or event.

If a customer calls up screaming mad at the terrible service she received on her computer, don't softly and calmly whisper that you are concerned. She won't feel your concern as very genuine. Raise your voice and exclaim that you are very concerned also and that you are going to get to the bottom of this. By screaming at the outside event or problem, you will be perceived as caring and truly empathetic—and you will give the customer an opportunity to ventilate her emotions (which can be one of the most important functions of the call).

By the way, the brokerage house we worked with had increasing sales from the first day onward as they coached their sales representatives to pace the speech volume of their prospects and customers. As an added benefit, the sales representatives found that they had more energy to make additional calls when they gave up the screaming ploy and that their self-image as professionals improved.

Pacing has many benefits besides increased personal power and increased ability to build trust and rapport.

IDIOSYNCRATIC AND PRIVATE LANGUAGE

Neuro-linguistic research has shown that each of us thinks with his or her own private mental language. While a few people are aware of how they talk to themselves, most are not. The closest glimpse they get of this internal processing is in their dreams.

Hearing a recording of one's own voice and speech can also reveal idiosyncratic ways of thinking. Some of these are almost inborn or genetic, as every member of a family will speak in that way. Others are acquired through years of experience at working or living in a particular environment.

The idiosyncratic language of some people, for example, is very feeling-, action-, and touch-oriented. The person may talk about having to "go out on a limb" to get a purchase order approved, or being "stuck in a rut" with a current supplier. Research has revealed that top sales producers intuitively switch to feeling- or action-oriented language when selling to this type of person. It is no wonder they are so successful! The language of their own private thought processes, which is reflected in spoken language, will encounter minimal resistance and will be seen as making sense.

Long years of conditioning or working within one industry develop particular habits of thought. In your tickler file make notes about the hobbies, special interests, and work specializations of your prospects and customers. If you are selling bonds to a retired military career man, for example, talk about "working your way through a battlefield of investment options" or the dangers of an investment that "bombs," "destroying" your portfolio. If you are selling whole life insurance to a farmer, talk about "planting a seed that will grow into a tree of protection in the future," or of "weeding out the unwanted insurance plans."

You may feel a bit self-conscious at first in using such a range of phrases. This is because, like everyone else, you are locked into your own private idiosyncratic language. Speaking someone else's language requires you to enter their world, which will be somewhat unfamiliar at first. The increased rapport, friendliness, and sales you will get from using the other person's private language will quickly convince you of the value of being flexible in this area. With practice, you will become more comfortable and you'll actually have fun speaking your clients' idiosyncratic languages.

PACING DIALECTS AND ACCENTS

It takes great skill to match customers' dialects and accents. Many top sales producers can match a few words only, unless they were born in another part of the country or in another country. We have encountered sales professionals in larger cities who have actually taken lessons in acting and voice to learn how to change their accents and dialects to match more closely those of customers.

Few people have the interest or inclination to invest the time and energy required to pace dialects and accents.

Remember that there is always something to pace and some way to get rapport and trust with anyone you meet. If you have an ear for dialect and the desire to master this aspect of communication, it is best to pick a few easy words and build from there.

DEVELOPING A POWERFUL VOICE

We have greatly improved our understanding of what makes a powerful voice. Older forms of sales, management, and self-confidence training taught students to speak in a loud, sometimes booming voice. This was supposed to show the speaker to be self-confident and someone whose orders are to be followed.

In professional selling or management, the goal is not to bully or overwhelm the other person. The aim is not to get the person merely to comply but to cooperate actively. This is at the heart of repeat business. A loud, booming voice is simply loud. Not necessarily perceived as self-confident, it occasionally succeeds in having someone place an order, but it is doubtful that much trust or rapport will result.

The most powerful voice is one that builds great trust quickly, one that invites no resistance. It is the voice that carries the message straight to the mark.

By pacing speech tempo and volume, you will be noticeably ahead of your competitors. Other characteristics of voice include pitch, rate, tonality, rhythm, and timbre. We experience considerable success in raising sales profits in client companies by having them practice these skills.

3

Handling Diverse Opinions, Beliefs and Objections

None of us really knows the nature of the world or the nature of reality. We take in a limited range of information through our senses and then form mental maps, which correspond to greater or lesser degrees with the outside world. These mental maps become our reality. Whatever information has filtered in through our senses and has been psychologically distorted by our past experiences, we call truth.

What types of friends do you have? Do you share many of the same opinions and beliefs? Imagine this scenario: You have invited one of your best friends to your home for dinner.

"I didn't know you liked steaks," she exclaims. "That's OK. I wasn't really hungry anyway. I'll sit over here and listen to some music until you've finished eating. Gee, most of your albums are country music. And there is a lot of Willie Nelson. He is *so* overrated. Really, a no-talent bum. I can't stand him. I'm surprised you paid money for this junk."

Is this a likely occurrence? Do your friends often attack your opinions, values, and beliefs?

Think about war. People will kill and die for opinions and beliefs. Do you think it might be important to understand their role in the sales and management worlds?

HOW TO BE HONEST

Few people are less successful or ultimately less liked than the phony. You know the type—the overagreeable placater who

39

seems to go along with everything you say and who just happens to like everything you like:

"Judy, that's a gorgeous jacket you are wearing. And I was just admiring these art prints you have on the walls. You could be a decorator for *House Beautiful!* Hey, I ran into your secretary at the store, and do you know what? She told me you are the best boss she's ever had!"

These overagreeables have good intentions, and they also have a basic understanding of the power of personal belief systems. They know it is dangerous to attack someone's belief systems because you are attacking their reality. What they need to learn is how to pace belief systems tactfully and skillfully.

You can pace the belief systems of another person while being honest and true to your own through use of the "101 percent principle." Helen Hoyer, one of the top real estate agents in the Pacific Northwest, uses it intuitively.

Helen specializes in selling large ranch properties. As in many forms of sales, once her prospects get to know the salesperson better, they frequently bring up emotional and potentially dangerous topics such as politics and religion. One example shows how Helen skillfully paces diverse opinions and beliefs without compromising her integrity.

She was showing a ranch property to a wealthy and vocal Ronald Reagan supporter. This was indeed a challenge as Helen did not happen to be a Reagan supporter herself. She knew, however, that it would be suicide to disagree flatly with her prospect's belief system. Helen selected something she truly admired in Reagan and talked about how healthy he looked and his impressive oratory skills. She showed much enthusiasm in stating these opinions, which she does genuinely hold. The rancher shifted over to the discussion of these areas of agreement and completely forgot about Reagan's economic and political programs. Their relationship flourished, and the rancher later purchased two properties from Helen.

Helen refocused the attention of the rancher's mind by selecting a relatively small area of agreement (the 1 percent) and then endorsing it with 100 percent of her enthusiasm. This is where the title of the 101 percent principle comes in. Opinions and beliefs are complex, and there is always some part of another person's value system you can agree with. The 101 percent principle reminds us to do this. Frequently, there is 20 or 30 percent we can agree with. Once this area of agreement is found, enthusiasm comes into play.

Building trust and rapport is part art and part science. It does require some work, but all efforts are richly rewarded. What is much simpler and easier to do is to destroy trust and rapport. A recipe for doing so is to disagree with another person's beliefs and values.

It is important to make a distinction here between the more emotional beliefs and beliefs about product features and other facts. Beliefs about subjects such as politics, religion, the women's movement, affirmative action, and other strongly held opinions are part of a person's ego system. You cannot attack these beliefs without also attacking the individual and his or her self-esteem. To some, this is almost unforgivable. Beliefs about product features, advantages, and benefits can also be profitably paced, but it is safer to lead the individual to new areas of understanding since these are relatively less connected to the ego. How this is done is described in Chapter 9.

Once trust and rapport have been established, it is proper to face the inevitable differences involved in selling or influencing. The individual who avoids facing differences becomes a semiprofessional people pleaser who runs the risk of being viewed as spineless and weak. The super-agreeable person forgets that respect is an important ingredient in influence management. Customers, subordinates, and peers often expect to be led and to be given recommendations. When this is lacking, disappointment follows.

What of those rare occasions when it seems impossible to agree with even 1 percent of another person's beliefs? It is not, even in this situation, necessary to lie. Research has found that top sales producers say something like, "Jim, I am certain that if I were in your position I would feel exactly the same way."

This seemingly simple method is powerful, useful and true. If you had their parents, had gone to the same schools, had the same friends, read the same books, and shared all of the other background experiences of work and marriage, you would be likely to have the same viewpoints. Therefore, you can honestly say, "I see and appreciate where you are coming from, and if I were in your position I would probably feel the same way. I respect your opinion." You are also communicating that respect to the individual. That is ultimately what most people want and need to hear. You can sell to people whose beliefs are very different from your own.

What is the key to skill and tact in dealing with people? There is always some way to build trust and rapport and a valuable feeling of agreement. If you cannot agree with opinions and beliefs, you can pace the speech rate and volume and the body language of the other person. Top salespeople give the customer the feeling of being understood, supported, and reinforced. They accomplish this by thoroughly pacing the other person on many different conscious and subconscious levels simultaneously. Through pacing it is always possible to build more trust and rapport.

CONTROLLING THE FUTURE

Would you like to have the ability to influence in some ways how people see the future? The techniques of future pacing can give you that ability.

Today much of the world is future-oriented. Japan is generally perceived as being one of the most future-oriented countries, followed closely by the United States. With the advent of more sophisticated and more rapid communications networks, something that happens in one part of the world is instantly transmitted to all other parts. Trends spread with increasing rapidity. One recent best-seller gave us a glimpse of the future by examining mega-trends.

The future can be paced, matched, or mirrored in both oral and written communication:

> You are now reading about new dimensions in professional sales communication. Many of them may strike you as fascinating and potentially very useful. You are already learning how you might apply some of them with your customers day after day. As you do so, you will become more and more skilled, and it will become easier and easier for you to succeed. Your influence will grow, and it will be

easier for you to afford more of the things you want. You will also have better relationships with more and more people. It is within your grasp now. You can already see this coming true in your future.

In this example, we started by pacing some undeniably true facts about the future: You *are* now reading about some new dimensions in professional sales communications. We then bridge into the future. Why do people relate to this type of future-pacing language? It is built, first of all, upon a bedrock of pacing statements about the future. Then it leads into general statements about the future. What is said has already happened and has become true for many other people—so why not for you?

It is important that future-pacing statements be kept general, especially at first. The minds of your listeners will customize the words you use automatically to give them more personal meanings. Use statements that fit the individual and are impossible to disagree with. Talk about pleasant events and enjoyable developments. It is wise to suggest that people can grow and change and learn. This is one of the most important programming messages any salesperson or manager can give. Concentrating on pleasant messages also ensures that your customer or prospect will want to continue listening to what you have to say.

Here are some examples of other future-pacing statements you can use:

- "Some day you are going to retire and…"
- "Someday your children are going to become adults and…"
- "Some day you will probably want to expand this factory and…"
- "Some day you will want to take it a little easy and…"
- "Given your energy and intelligence, you can look forward to…"
- "Grasp a vision of how you want your plant to look in the future."

You know you are getting through by using future-pacing statements when you notice your prospects and customers making such gestures as slight head nods or saying, "Yes, yes" to your statements. Capitalize on these feelings of agreement. Use them as stepping stones to a land of new understandings.

With practice, almost anything can be future-paced. Become a collector of information about your customer, his or her work, hobbies, family, interests, likes, and dislikes. This will make it almost effortless to talk accurately about his or her future. Astrologers and psychics have long known the secret of future pacing. It is not an arcane art, but a practical one that can be used effectively in even the most conservative business environments.

The key to future pacing is to speak in meaningful and sincere ways. Future-pacing lines casually thrown out lose much of their effectiveness. However, the president can get on nationwide television and say, "We are facing a great crisis in the near future with our Social Security program," and get millions of heads to nod in unison. The statement itself contains no new information and could be banal. But when meaningfully pronounced, it is more effective in building trust and rapport and in leading the way for his new proposal than more factual, detailed, and ultimately riskier statements.

As your customer sends signals of agreement, begin leading him or her into the new areas of discussion. If you encounter any resistance, simply go back to what was previously agreed upon. Reestablish the trust, look again at his or her future, regenerate the good feelings, and proceed confidently toward closing the deal.

4

How to Offer
Your Listener
Irresistible Information

THE COLD READER

My friend Irma has her fortune read every year, and she is amazed at how much fortune tellers know about her. Yet Irma is no dummy. Instead of visiting one, she consults three or four in different parts of the city. Invariably, the tea-leaf reader, the palm reader, and the astrologer give her readings that are so similar that they leave her breathless. At the last go-around they told her she was going to get married in March. How is that for coincidence among soothsayers who don't even know one another?

Coincidence? Well, not exactly. These fortune tellers are really cold readers, sophisticated mind readers who convince clients they have never met that they know everything about their personality and problems. In that respect they share a most valuable asset with the peak performers of the sales world, those men and women who have developed their intuitive skills to sonar precision. You, the serious sales professional, now have a tool at your mental fingertips that enables you to develop deliberately your own intuitive awareness and to program your customers to give you the expected buying response. You may not want to be a cold reader, but you can become a master communicator.

Why do some people like listening to records, while others would rather curl up with a book and still others spend their free time jogging? Why do some people need to be told "I love you," when others see it in a look and nothing need be said? Why can some people follow verbal directions, while others have to have everything carefully spelled out and diagrammed? Why do some people recognize your face after 20 years, but not your name, and vice versa?

These differences seem to have little to do with intelligence or education, according to research. This mind-blowing discovery suggests that all people have a preferred communication channel—seeing, hearing, or action–feeling–movement. To put it another way, some of us are visual, others are auditory, and still others are kinesthetic. What's important to you as a sales professional is that there is a profound difference among the types of information your customers prefer and react to. When you determine your customer's favorite channel, you're well on the way to selling him or her.

If the prospect is highly visual ("That looks good to me. That's not clear. Can you shed some light on the subject?"), use pacing and visual language. He or she will understand you faster, because you speak his or her language. If he or she is sound-oriented ("It sounds good to me. That rings a bell."), be respectful and speak his or her language. Not only will the prospect trust you, but what you say will also make instant sense to him or her.

If the prospect has a preference for action–feeling–movement words ("I can't get a grip on that. I don't want to go out on a limb."), again speak his or her language. He or she will be delighted.

When you are able to detect and pace your customer's speech clues, you'll be well rewarded. Because communication channels are a significant part of pacing, they will be extensively treated later.

That each of us has a favorite type of communication channel has profound significance for professional salespeople. On what basis do people choose a product? Some rely on what they see, others on what they hear, and still others on what they feel. To increase your success with all of them, it's important to learn how to spot them and speak their language.

By using their communication wavelength, you make it easy for them to take in, absorb, and believe what you are saying. If you perceive the world differently from the way they do and unconsciously communicate that, many of your best points will be scattered or lost. All you can tell is that the listener was not paying attention. You have to recognize and react to the information and stimuli that the customer finds important. Failure to do so is somewhat like the blind selling the deaf. Information that may seem relevant to you may be meaningless to your prospect. There is something intuitive in the way great ministers, lawyers, entertainers, statesmen, psychologists, and salespeople relate to others. Their radar system causes them to develop an awareness about others, to which they react automatically. Until recently this extra dimension was unknown. Modeling, a new research technique using high-speed cameras and sound tracks, is proving that people pick up telltale signals in others' faces, voices, and behavior. They process and react to these signals in a flash, so that they can establish that critical trust and rapport between themselves and the other person. This information is now at hand and can be learned by any professional salesperson who is interested in becoming a master.

Unschooled people assume that everyone understands the world the way they do. Experienced salespeople know better. They can't help but recognize that people do not see, hear, and feel everything in the same way. The problem is what to do about it.

In contrast, champion salespeople not only know that people are different, but also know how to take advantage of these differences. That is what makes them the persuasive communicators and effective professionals they are. Often, their know-how is intuitive, and they are not able to explain all of the skillful things they do. Abraham Maslow calls them "unconscious competents." This is why some of the best salespeople can't teach others to sell.

When you deliver your sales message of substance and use the customer's preferred communication channel, your message will carry maximum impact. The customer will find it stimulating and enjoyable.

How can you determine your favorite channel? One way is to think of what you prefer to do in your free time. That will give you a rough idea about the information and activities you favor. It's also an indication of how you prefer to learn and communicate.

No matter how sincere and caring you are in your sales presentation—no matter how much expertise, energy, or product knowledge you may display—unless you speak the customer's language, your sales performance will suffer, and much of what you do will have been wasted.

In Figures 4–1, 4–2, and 4–3, you will find the Information Checklist designed to assist salespeople in discovering their preferred ways of relating to the world. Notice the 20 items in each of the three communication channels. Put a check next to each item that is basically true for you. Don't think about the item too much—your first guess is probably your most accurate. If an item stumps you, ask your spouse or a good friend. It is likely that they can answer this item about you quickly and accurately.

Once you have read all of the items and checked the ones that are true for you, add up the number of checks for each of the orientations (visual, auditory and feeling–movement–touch). You may be surprised which communication channel is strongest and weakest.

Why do cafeteria lines move so slowly? Why do kids ponder the ice cream tubs in their 27-flavor splendor? Because they check out their sense of taste. Not only that, but they also check out the appearance and what other people may say about a dish. Even the sense of touch can be important. If it weren't, we would all eat baby food.

Travelers report that in other countries people are more taste and smell-oriented. This is a matter of culture and early training, which results in our communication preferences in the first place. The information channels of taste and smell have not been as much developed in our society. There are some reasons for this. Human speech seems to give the best rendition in describing what we see and what we do, but experiences increasing difficulties in describing sound, taste, and smell. Even the number of descriptive words in our language are fewer in the last three communication channels. We often use words from the language of feeling, seeing, and sound to strengthen our descriptions.

Beer is full-bodied or light (feeling). Perfume and after-shave lotion are described as intoxicating or macho. Our society has not been able to develop and perfect these two channels as a reliable communication tool.

Figure 4–1 INFORMATION PREFERENCE CHECKLIST
VISUAL ORIENTATION

_____ 1. On an evening when I don't have anything else to do, I like to watch TV.

_____ 2. I use visual images to remember names.

_____ 3. I like to read books and magazines.

_____ 4. I prefer to get written instructions from my boss rather than oral ones.

_____ 5. I write lists to myself of things I have to do.

_____ 6. I follow recipes closely when I am cooking.

_____ 7. I can easily put together models and toys if I have written instructions.

_____ 8. When it comes to playing games, I prefer word games like Scrabble and Password.

_____ 9. I am very concerned about the way I look.

_____ 10. I like to go to art exhibits and museum displays.

_____ 11. I keep a diary or a written record of what I have been doing.

_____ 12. I often admire the photographs and artwork used in advertisements.

_____ 13. I review for a test by writing down a summary of all pertinent points.

_____ 14. I can find my way around a new city easily if I have a map.

_____ 15. I like to keep my house very neat-looking.

_____ 16. I see two or more films each month.

_____ 17. I think less highly of a person if he or she does not dress nicely.

_____ 18. I like to watch people.

_____ 19. I always get scratches and dents repaired quickly on my car.

_____ 20. I think fresh flowers really brighten up a home or office.

_____ Total score for Visual Orientation

Figure 4–2
AUDITORY ORIENTATION

_____ 1. On an evening when I don't have anything else to do, I like to listen to music.

_____ 2. To remember someone's name, I will repeat it to myself over and over again.

_____ 3. I enjoy long conversations.

_____ 4. I prefer having my boss explain something to me orally rather than in a memo.

_____ 5. I like talk shows and interview shows on radio and television.

_____ 6. I use rhyming words to help me remember things.

_____ 7. I am a good listener.

_____ 8. I prefer to keep up with the news by listening to the radio rather than by reading.

_____ 9. I talk to myself a lot.

_____ 10. I prefer to listen to a cassette tape of some material rather than to read it.

_____ 11. I feel bad when my car sounds funny (has knocks, pings, etc.).

_____ 12. I can tell a lot about a person by the sound of his or her voice.

_____ 13. I buy a lot of albums and prerecorded tapes.

_____ 14. I review for a test by reading my notes aloud or by talking with other people.

_____ 15. I would rather give a talk than write a paper on the same topic.

_____ 16. I enjoy going to concerts and musical events.

_____ 17. People sometimes accuse me of talking too much.

_____ 18. When I am in a strange city, I like to stop at a gas station to get directions.

_____ 19. I talk to my dog or cat.

_____ 20. I talk aloud to myself when I'm solving a math problem.

_____ Total score for Auditory Orientation

Figure 4–3
FEELING–MOVEMENT–TOUCH ORIENTATION

_____	1. I like to exercise.
_____	2. When I am blindfolded, I can distinguish items by touch.
_____	3. When there is music on, I can't help but tap my feet.
_____	4. I am an outdoors person.
_____	5. I am well coordinated.
_____	6. I have a tendency to gain weight.
_____	7. I buy some clothes because I like the way the material feels.
_____	8. I like to pet animals.
_____	9. I touch people when I am talking with them.
_____	10. When I was learning to type, I learned the touch system easily.
_____	11. I was held and touched a lot when I was a child.
_____	12. I enjoy playing sports more than watching them.
_____	13. I like taking a hot bath at the end of a day.
_____	14. I really enjoy getting massages.
_____	15. I am a good dancer.
_____	16. I belong to a gym or health spa.
_____	17. I like to get up and stretch frequently.
_____	18. I can tell a lot about a person by the way he or she shakes hands.
_____	19. If I've had a bad day, my body gets very tense.
_____	20. I enjoy crafts, handworks, and/or building things.
_____	**Total score for Feeling–Movement–Touch Orientation**

What were your scores on the checklists? Were you aware that you had a favorite communication channel?

TV commercials appeal to one or more of the five senses:

- See (the white teeth)
- Hear (the crunchy potato chips)
- Feel or touch (the soft skin or the tissues)
- Taste (the light beer)
- Smell (the fragrance of the soap)

Charles deGaulle, president of France, held important discussions while walking with his visitors. The physical activity was the sparkplug for generating his best thoughts and conversations. Color him feeling–movement–action. The same holds true for the thousands of businesspeople who pace back and forth while dictating.

Contrast this with people who do best by writing out their thoughts before a meeting—the visuals—and compare this with people who prefer to use tape recorders instead—the auditory.

THE SIGNIFICANCE OF COMMUNICATION CHANNELS

You now know whether you exhibit visual, auditory, or action–feeling–movement tendencies. Just as you have a dominant tendency, so do your customers. The question is, are you sensitive to theirs and do you know how to use it to make more successful presentations?

The significance of communication channels cannot be overestimated. Because the senses of smell and taste do not often enter into sales situations, we are limited to understanding the world through our eyes, our ears, and our sense of action–feeling–movement. Think of what this means: Your customer is paying attention to only about seven things, and the majority of these may be visual, sound, or feeling. What if you are highly action–feeling–movement-oriented and you stress these aspects to a customer who is visual? Unless you operate on their channel, to the visual something "won't look right," to the auditory it "won't sound right," and to the kinesthetic it "won't feel right." In the next chapters you will learn how to recognize and speak the language that makes the most sense to your customers.

Now that you recognize which sensory system you prefer, you know which ones you have to strengthen. For example, if you are visual, you live in a visual world. You sketch and draw well. You pick up visual details. You probably form quick judgments of people by the way they look. You can glance at photographs and immediately form opinions about what you like and dislike. You may daydream frequently or have vivid night dreams. While your visual sense is highly developed, your abilities to appreciate the worlds of sound and action–feeling–movement will be somewhat more limited by comparison to it. This imbalance limits your sales performance.

Have you ever known a couple in which one partner complained that the other "never listens to what I'm saying"? And the other one says, "We just don't see eye to eye." These people live in different worlds, one visual and one auditory. Marriage counselors have to deal with this problem all the time. Don't give it a chance to crop up in your sales work.

You can prevent that by expanding your sensory awareness. Work on your inferior functions. If you are visual, work on appreciating sounds and action–feeling–movement. If you are sound-oriented, strengthen your visual and feeling–movement senses. If you live in a world of action–feeling–movement, develop your visual sense and your ear for auditory information.

As you consciously expand your ability to communicate, you will discover a new world of experience opening up to you. Hear food as you eat it, feel the texture of the fabric, look closely at your customer as you listen to him or her talk. Top producers do not allow themselves to be locked into one way of experiencing the world. They strive to increase their appreciation for all types of information.

There are a number of rewards for those who are aware of the richness of the information that surrounds us. You never run out of things to talk about or sell, because you're in the here and now. You are never bored. There is always something to appreciate. You will be less self-conscious, since you will be tuned into so many things besides yourself. Perhaps most importantly, you will be a much more powerful, flexible, and successful salesperson.

5

Discovering
Your Listener's
Information Preference

VISUAL LANGUAGE

Some people never forget a face. My son, back from Colorado for our traditional family reunion at Christmastime, entered a leather apparel store in the community where he had gone to grade school.

"Hi, Tom," said the owner. "It's been a long time."

Tom was dumbfounded and a little embarrassed.

"Do I know you?" asked Tom.

"Sure you do. I'm Ken Eaton. We went to grade school together."

"Oh, now I do," said Tom. "I remember your name." They hadn't seen or heard of each other since they were kids 22 years before.

Ken, owner and founder of that store, is visually oriented. In his business, where an eye for fashion and fit is important, that is a good thing. He also remembers people, their faces and names, another visual characteristic. Tom is not visual. More people recognize and remember him than vice versa. He remembered Ken and warmed to him once he heard his name.

John Reichard was a fraternity president who seemed to get a lot done in little time. To him everything was "no problem." He received superior grades in his four years at college, yet never burned the midnight oil as most of us had to do. In fact, he didn't seem to strain himself to get those grades.

Was John a better thinker and student than the others? Did he have a quicker grasp of the situation? Perhaps he did; perhaps he didn't. At least we never particularly seemed to notice. But one thing was true: John had what is called a photographic memory. As he explained, he could read some chapters in a book and write down verbatim what he had read the next day. After an especially important exam, one of the professors challenged him and put him to a test. John readily agreed and won. He was extremely visual. He had an eidetic memory.

Raphael, one of the world's great painters, did much of his work from memory. He was supposed to have said, "I just think about it and put in on canvas." Caricaturists and mimics quickly sense the essential characteristic of their subjects and imitate them dead to rights. They're supremely good observers.

"How can this help me?" you ask. By keen observing and listening, you can pace other people's favorite communication channel so that you speak the same language. You can also follow the familiar maxim of learning specialists, who have known for years that hearing something is good; hearing and seeing is better; and hearing, seeing, and doing is best of all.

Observe Your Customer's Eye Movements

When talking with you, visually oriented customers will frequently look up or allow their eyes to pan from left to right. These eye movements are associated with visualization and mean that the customer is seeing with his or her mind's eye. This person uses his or her memory and imagination in a visual way. Other signs of visualization include frequent blinking, closing the eyes, and a glassy or unfocused look.

Listen for Visual Language

Customers who speak the visual language use the following words frequently:

An eyeful	Beyond a shadow of a doubt	Clear
Analyze		Clearcut
Angle	Bird's-eye view	Clue
Appears	Bright	Cognizant
Aspect	Clarity	Conspicuous

Demonstrate	Look	Recognize
Dim view	Make a scene	Scrutinize
Discern	Mental image	See
Dream	Mental picture	See red
Examine	Mind's eye	See to it
Eye to eye	Naked eye	Shortsighted
Flash	Notice	show
Focus	Obscure	Showoff
Foresee	Observe	Sight
Get an image	Obvious	Sight for sore eyes
Get a perspective	Outlook	Sign
Glance	Outstanding	Sketchy
Hazy idea	Paint a picture	Stare
Hindsight	Peep	Staring off into space
Horizon	Perception	Survey
Horse of a different color	Perspective	Telltale sign
	Photographic memory	Tunnel vision
Idea		Up-front
Illusion	Picture	Vague
Illustrate	Pinpoint	View
Image	Plain	Vision
In light of	Plainly see	Watch
In view of	Pretty as a picture	Well-defined
Inspect	Read	Witness

Observe Voice, Breathing, Body Language, and Rate of Speech

Customers who are highly visual tend to breathe high up in the chest and have a more highly pitched tone of voice. They often speak in rapid bursts, tend to be thinner in body build, and often dress better than others in their economic range.

Working With Visuals

To sell successfully to a visual requires using visual words in your sales presentation, inviting the prospect to use his or her mind's eye. For example: "Imagine how these plants will look in a year from now." "Can you see the expression on your wife's face when you give her this ring?" "Picture the increased productivity you will have with this new computer system." Make liberal use of brochures, photographs, visual aids, and, where appropriate, films and videotapes. They fix the customer's attention, so that it is much harder for him or her to daydream about things unrelated to the product or service. Since you are using the prospect's natural language, he or she gets a clear understanding of your product or service and relates to you easily.

Numerous studies have shown that we tend to like people who are like ourselves. Employees who are like the boss are the first ones hired and the first ones promoted. Salespeople who are perceived as being "like I am" by the customer are trusted, and trust is the basis for successful human communication.

If all customers, except the blind, are able to see and appreciate sales brochures and visual aspects of a product, why shouldn't we use visual words and presentation material with everyone equally? Interesting question, negative answer. We shouldn't because some people are primarily sound-oriented or action–feeling–oriented. Later sections of this book will show you how to distinguish among different types of customers and how to speak persuasively to each. All human beings, regardless of intelligence, have a limited attention span and can easily become bored or overwhelmed. As a sales professional, it is crucial that you understand this fact and know how to use it. If your customer speaks the visual language and shows other signs of being visual, use the visual words given on the preceding page. Don't burden him or her with sound-oriented words or feeling-oriented words, at least not in the early stages of the presentation. In a similar vein, when your customer is either sound- or feeling-oriented, avoid starting your sales presentation with visual language.

Why Move from the Visual to Another Communication Channel?

One reason is to have your customers experience more of your products or services. After trust and rapport are built, you may wish to shift into the world of sounds or feelings with them. Some people unconsciously ignore much of the world around them. They prefer the visual because it's easiest for them. They miss the whole world of hearing and feeling, because they did not develop those capacities in themselves. Both you and they stand to gain a lot once you direct them to the hearing and feeling aspects of your products and services. As a sales technique, it's powerful, because it has an emotional impact on the customer and becomes an event not easily forgotten. It's a new experience for him or her. You'll find more information on how to do that effectively in Chapter 9.

A second reason for moving from the visual to another communication channel is to allow you to penetrate the armor of rigid-minded thinkers, people who, like horses, seem to have blinders on. Narrow in their viewpoint or fixated on one particular detail, they have dug themselves a visual trench. They have more than blind spots in the usual sense. They have blind areas. They have no peripheral vision. As a consequence there's a lot around them, to which they are not receptive.

You get through to these customers by switching from visual to sound or action–feelings. It induces gentle confusion in their minds and makes them want to know more. You have brought about a change by redirecting their attention and making it easier for them to think about and experience your product or service in a new way.

How to Introduce Another Communication Channel

It's important to distinguish between open-minded and rigid people when switching communication channels. With open-minded people the transition is smooth and imperceptible to enlarge their experiences (bridging techniques). With rigid-minded customers the purpose is to startle them by making a sudden switch to the language of hearing and feeling. It's as if you had spun them around for a minute and now present them with a map to get reoriented. Instead of telling them they are rigid or that you are frustrated by them, both of which are useless, they'll suddenly realize that they have only looked north.

AUDITORY LANGUAGE

Ever wonder why most inventors are men? Or why for half a century the world's greatest pianists and violinists came from Odessa in Russia? Or why for a time the best American weight lifters lived in York, Pennsylvania? Or why most comedians are short? Or why East Germany wins a high percentage of Olympic medals, even though its population is only 17 million?

The answer is programming, exposing talented people to intensive skills training and motivation. Many comedians reminisce that the only equalizer with their taller and stronger schoolmates was not a gun but their quick wit. Can you imagine a tougher audience? What are we learning from this once again? It's conditioning; it's programming. Whether we are visual, auditory, or feeling- and action-oriented is largely a matter of conditioning.

Conditioning is effective. The marathon is no longer the domain of men. Women have begun to be world-class competitors. Even the iron-man contest consisting of the marathon followed by an endurance swim and a 50-mile bicycle race counts a woman among its five best competitors.

How about selling? The top Cadillac salesperson in a 4 million population area is a woman.

Why do some people prefer the auditory communication channel? They're programmed that way.

Parents will tell you that their daughters talked earlier and better than their sons. People don't raise eyebrows about the ability of girls to verbalize better, or to pick up foreign languages faster or remember poems, songs, and advertising jingles more quickly. Boys are not expected to be as articulate. An old Italian proverb says, "Males do; females talk." Does it imply that one is more predisposed to a certain communication channel? Yes, it does. Could we change it if we wanted to? Yes, we could.

Look at Albert Einstein. His family thought he might be retarded, because he still couldn't talk at age four. Einstein was not auditory. He was visual in the extreme. Yet he learned to be a relatively good violinist in his time.

Observe Your Customer's Eye Movements

When we talked about the visual, we said to observe their eye movements. Now that we talk about sound-oriented people, will we say to watch their ears? Of course not. Even with auditory people, the eye movements provide the clues. Eye movements are never random. They are the signals of how a person recalls scenes from the past, stores memory (tape loops), talks to himself or herself, and thinks. Customers who are primarily sound-oriented will, when you watch them closely, occasionally look left and down. Top-flight salespeople, keen observers of people, use this vital clue to tune in to the frequency band of their customers for clearer communication.

Observe Body Language and Voice

Think of the brain as a computer program and the eyes as a video screen. In addition to eye movements, the auditory program is "on" when a customer's hand touches his or her face, taps his or her chin, or rubs his or her cheek. The customer is likely to be in the so-called telephone position, during which he or she is in an internal dialogue mode, which means he or she talks to himself or herself without moving his or her lips. Studies show that this is true even in cultures where there are no telephones. The next time you find yourself resting your chin on your hands, check yourself by asking, "What am I telling myself?" After doing this a few times you will develop a high degree of awareness of your internal dialogue and will be able to determine whether you programmed yourself positively or negatively.

Customers who are primarily sound-oriented will speak in an even and pleasant voice register. You can occasionally hear them hum, whistle, or make clicking sounds.

Listen for Auditory Language

Those preferring the auditory (sound) language use the following words frequently:

Amplify	Articulate	Audible
Announce	Ask	Blabbermouth

Boisterous	Invite	Shout
Call	Keynote speaker	Shrill
Clear as a bell	Listen	Silence
Clearly expressed	Loud	Sound
Comment on	Loud and clear	Speak
Communicate	Manner of speaking	Speechless
Describe in detail	Mention	Squeal
Discuss	Mutter	State
Dissonant	Noise	Suggest
Divulge	Oral	Talk
Earful	Outspoken	Tattletale
Earshot	Overhear	Tell
Enunciate	Pay attention to	To tell the truth
Exclaim	Power of speech	Tone
Express yourself	Proclaim	Tongue-tied
Give an account of	Pronounce	Tune
Give me your ear	Purrs like a kitten	Tuned in or tuned out
Gossip	Quiet	Unheard of
Grant an audience	Quoted	Utter
Hear	Rap session	Utterly
Heard voices	Remark	Vocal
Hidden message	Report	Voice
Hold your tongue	Rings a bell	Voiced an opinion
Hush	Roar	Well-informed
Idle talk	Rumor	Within hearing range
Inform	Say	Word for word
Inquire	Scream	
Interview	Screech	

Working with Auditory People

Learn to speak the language of the sound-oriented customer. Do so by using the sound words above. Suggest to the customer that he or she tune in to what other people say about what he or she bought. "Your neighbors will talk about your noiseless lawn mower that you can use at 6:00 A.M. on Saturdays." Or, "Your boss will compliment you for your good judgment in selecting a word processor rather than a typewriter."

Inform your sound-oriented customers what experts, trade journals, and other customers say about your product. "*Consumer's Report* says it is the best buy on the market." When called for, give your sound-oriented customer the phone numbers of two or three satisfied customers. When he or she hears what these people say, it will have a positive impact.

Speak the prospect's language. It sounds natural to him or her and intuitively makes sense. When you quote a person he or she respects, it is effective because this plugs directly into his or her communication channel. Appeal to his or her built-in preference for this kind of information by commenting on the sounds of your product, if it has any: "Listen to the way these doors latch. Hardly audible." "Listen to this new plate stamping machine. Twice as quiet as the one you have now." When you speak the sound language used by your sound-oriented customers, they will feel you understand them. You will be in harmony.

These sections on visual, auditory, and feeling languages deal with building trust and rapport with customers. Trust is the basis for all successful human communication and of all successful sales work. Matching the customer's language preference is the fastest way known to build trust effectively. Studies confirm that we tend to like people who are like we are. They show that the first employees to be hired, and the last ones fired, are those most like the boss. It may not be fair, but that is the way the world is. To be an effective and trusted salesperson, you communicate to the customer that you are like him or her. Using auditory language with a sound-oriented customer unmistakably communicates this.

All customers, except those who are deaf, are able to hear and appreciate auditory information. Shouldn't we then use the auditory language with all customers equally? No, we shouldn't. Some customers are primarily visual. Others are feeling-oriented. The world is so complex that no human being can pay equal amounts of attention to visual, auditory, and feeling or action information.Everyone has a favorite communication channel. This helps us simplify the complexity of the world. It helps customers make purchase decisions. The truth is that customers don't pay equal attention to all aspects of a product or service.

The auditory language does not work well with a customer who is visual- or feeling-oriented. It does not seem right or feel right to these customers. You may have inadvertently been using auditory language on some of your visual or action–feeling customers. You would tend to do this if you yourself are sound-oriented. Neither you nor your customer may have known what went wrong—all you know is that something didn't look right, feel right, or sound right. And you didn't make the sale. It is time to increase your awareness of these language preferences among people, so that you can learn to speak their language.

There are times when you don't want to use the auditory language, or when it is best to use it sparingly.

When to Move Away from the Auditory Channel

After building trust and rapport, you may wish to switch to a different channel. Draw the prospect's attention to the world of visual information or the world of action–feeling. Some people are so sound-oriented that they tend to minimize the visual and action–feeling aspects of your product or service. At this very moment there are numberless salespeople whose own preferences about their product characteristics severely limit to whom they will sell successfully. Here is an illustration.

A few years ago, working with some of the Bell operating companies, I discovered a strong bias against all but the most functional telephones by some installation and repair people. They disliked the idea of design line telephones, feeling that they cost too much. They weren't aware that people buy for reasons altogether different from theirs. Once the truth of this took hold, literally hundreds of field personnel doubled, tripled, and quintupled their sales. They made a momentous discovery—people buy telephones for fun, or for decor, or for the sound of the chimes. Others buy for status reasons, or for protection in case of burglaries, or for convenience or increased privacy. This is where design line phones came in.

In order to reach more customers, you have to introduce other communication channels, such as the visual and action–feeling aspects of your product or service. Doing so is a very powerful sales technique, because you are actually opening up a new world of experience for this type of customer and for yourself. Be sensitive in doing it. Avoid an abrupt shift from the auditory language to another language. See Chapter 9, "Utilizing Bridging Techniques for Leading People" for details.

How to Introduce Another Communication Channel

Sometimes you will encounter a customer encumbered by such rigid thinking that he or she is trapped in his or her own narrow-minded beliefs. This customer is in a rut. It is very difficult to sell to such a person and top sales producers realize that it is occasionally necessary to change languages quickly. When expertly done, this unstructures the customer's rigid thinking, because it momentarily confuses the customer and creates the need for new information in him or her. You can then sell the customer on other aspects of your product, using visual or action–feeling language, and bring things to a successful close.

THE ACTION–FEELING LANGUAGE

No question about it, Americans are action-minded people. We may be passive participants, but we love to watch others in action. And we love statistics, especially in sports and sales. By latest count there are now more TV sets—90 million—than telephones—only 86 million. The telephone is a hearing medium, but TV is a triple medium: see, hear, and action–feeling. What is particularly interesting to us are the TV commercials, where, of course, the selling takes place. While A. C. Nielsen and others poll programs for their audience appeal, other companies rate the commercials for their ability to draw people into stores and showrooms. Sponsors are most interested in that kind of action.

By their very nature, all TV commercials are visual and auditory. But how they put their sales points across is the issue here. Watch some to see what and how they do it, and note their theme. "Reach out and touch someone" is action–feeling language, even though it means talking to someone on the telephone. "Go for it" is action–feeling language again and says, "Dial Channel 4 with enthusiasm." Or the tall-tale exchange between a fisherman and a lumberjack who reminisces, "When we worked in the great Sahara Forest," and his buddy interrupts with, "Sahara Forest—you mean Sahara Desert, don't you?" And he replies, "It is now." This is action–feeling language of the "can-you-top-this?" variety.

Action–feeling expressions abound in everyday language: "He is a man on the go." "They're on a fast track." "She is a mover and shaker." "Las Vegas—that's where the action is." "Keep your nose to the grindstone." "Your eye on the ball." "Your shoulder to the wheel." "Your foot in the door." "Your mind on your work." Some are old, some are not. All have gusto and verve. They get the adrenalin going, charge your batteries and your can-do spirit.

Americans are sold on action. When a rookie fell out of formation during the regulation 28-mile hike with a 60-pound pack in infantry basic training, and lay exhausted in a ditch by the side of a dusty road, someone was sure to taunt, "Don't just lie there—do pushups." This wry humor keenly signaled an understanding of action fixation.We are so saturated with action that we sometimes overlook the need to plan. Survival exercises, whether simulated or real, stress the need for clarity of thought and planning. Any certified scuba diver will agree that calm thinking in the face of danger is the key to survival 120 feet below sea level, while action induced by panic is often fatal.

People who dance well but couldn't begin to tell you how they do it are "naturals." Arthur Murray, who by his own admission was no natural, had to learn ballroom dancing the visual way and in the process was also able to teach all those who couldn't before.

The same is true for selling. Only 20 percent are "tell me" people, while 80 percent are "show me" people. And even then, only after repeatedly practicing the right way does any skill become a part of us. How can you distinguish an action–feeling customer from the others?

Observe Your Customer's Eye Movements

Action- and feeling-oriented customers frequently tend to look down and to the right, a characteristic that has scientifically been shown to be associated with sorting through one's feelings or getting in touch with one's feelings. Professional actors and actresses, when preparing for emotional scenes, tend to look down and to their right also. They also tend to do that in personal interviews on TV. During a recent television interview on "60 Minutes," the winner of the Vietnam War Memorial Design, Maya Linn, a 21-year-old art student from Yale, repeatedly looked down and to her right before answering Morley Safer's questions. She described how she arrived at the design and explained that she wanted to chisel in marble her feelings for the people who had made the ultimate sacrifice.

Listen For Action–Feeling Language

Customers who are strongly action–feeling-oriented use the following words frequently:

Active	Control	Forceful	Hand in hand
Affected	Cool	Foundation	Handle
All washed up	Cutting	Get a handle	Hang
Bearable	Depth	on	Hang in there
Bails down to	Effort	Get a load of	Know-how
Callous	Embrace	this	Lay your cards
Charge	Emotional	Get in touch	on the table
Chip off the	Experience	with	Light-headed
old block	Fall apart	Get the drift	Lukewarm
Cold	Feel	of	Lump
Come to grips	Firm	Get your goat	Moment of
with	Floating	Grasp	panic
Comfortable	Flow	Grip	Motion
Concrete	Flush	Grow	Move

Hard-headed	Not following	Shook	Swelling
Hassle	you	Slipped my	Tap
Head on	Panicky	mind	Tension
Heated	Pressure	Smooth	Throb
Heated	Pull some	Smooth	Tied up
argument	strings	operator	Tight
Heavy	Push	Snap	Tired
Hold	Respond	Soft	Too much
Hold it	Rough	Solid	hassle
Hold on	Rush	Sore	Topsy-turvy
Hot-headed	Seized	Stand for	Touch
Hunch	Sensation	Start from	Unbearable
Hurt	Sense	scratch	Unbeatable
Hustle	Sensitive	Stiff upper lip	Underhanded
Intuition	Set	Stir	Unsettled
Involve	Shallow	Stress	Warm
Keep your	Sharp	Structure	Wear
shirt on	Shift	Stuffed shirt	Weary
Muddled	Shock	Suffer	Whipped
		Support	Wince

Observe Voice, Breathing, Body Language, and Rate of Speech

Action–feeling people tend to breathe fully and deeply, using gestures when speaking. They tend to speak somewhat slowly in low and resonant voices and frequently touch their clothing or their bodies. People who have a muscular body build tend to be action–feeling persons. In their later years they have a tendency toward overweight. Those people also reveal themselves by their preferences in hobbies and their conversation and other interests. Customers who spend their free time in athletic games, sports, hunting, and fishing like action–feeling talk. Use this fact when selling to them. Speak the language of action and feeling.

Working With Action–Feeling Persons

To sell successfully to the action–feeling customer, use movement-, feeling-, and action-based words. Let the customer get a feel for your product or service, how it operates, handles, fits, or drives. "Experience the feeling of luxury you'll have driving this car." "Experience the feeling of control and efficiency you'll get from this computer system."

Involve your action–feeling customers physically whenever possible. Have them walk through the plant with you to experience unnecessary work stoppages first-hand. Make them sit down and type something on the keyboard. Let them touch the smooth finish. Have them operate the machinery early in the demonstration. Get them to drive the car or truck.

Richard Allen, Cessna's ultimate salesman, has been described as appealing to as many communication channels as possible. Early in his demonstration he gets the customer to see a plane take off and land, thus appealing to the sense of action or feeling, as well as to the visual and auditory channels.

Later these feelings are reinforced in a number of ways. He has the customer sit in the plane during takeoff and landing and involves him or her in other action–feeling experiences to appeal for greatest impact on his senses.

When it's not possible to put the customer through an actual experience, you have a choice among various desk-top demonstrations (as done in beer-tasting or laundry commercials) or talking about how other customers feel about using your product or service. It will be an advantage to you to quote their words or, even better, to refer to their comments in writing, particularly if they are well-known people in the industry or community.

Action–feeling customers will understand you more quickly and easily if you use the language that feels right and makes intuitive sense to them. Speaking their language makes it easy for them to grasp what you are saying, as a result of which they will feel most comfortable with you. You're their kind of person.

Speaking the customer's language is not only psychologically sound, but it is also considerate of what he or she finds easiest to internalize. When selling to an engineer, use engineering terms. This concept applies in equal measure to accountants, computer people, and others. When I use the language of your profession—your acronyms, your jargon, your symbols, your orientation—you'll find it easy to absorb the information and easy to relate to me.

Another illustration is the advantage of speaking in positive rather than negative terms. Psychologists tell us that negatives take longer to process, since we mentally take the positive and reverse it. For many people, double negatives are frustrating.

As explained earlier, we all have preferences for certain types of information. It is not possible for us, given our limited attention span, to pay equal attention to visual, auditory, and action–feeling aspects of reality. As children we develop preferences and biases to simplify our task of learning about the world and understanding it.

The action–feeling language works best with customers who have this kind of information preference. Clues have already been given about how these customers talk and look.

When to Move from the Action–Feeling Communication Channel

The only time the action–feeling channel does not work is when it is not used frequently enough. You cannot simply use two or three feeling words and then go back to visual or sound language patterns. You need to keep talking the language the customer understands.

Intelligent Confusion

There are times when you don't want the action–feeling language to work. If you have an extremely narrow-minded and highly biased customer, you may wish to speak in a different language to temporarily induce some confusion. This technique, as used by top salespeople, is effective in creating a need for new information in the customer. It is a powerful technique and must be used with care. Here is how it works.

If you are dealing with an action–feeling-oriented customer, shift into the visual or auditory gear exclusively. By using the other communication channels when talking about features, the customer will experience and think about them in new ways.

This technique is useful in unstructuring mental blocks of narrow-minded or biased customers. Of course, you don't want to change a narrow-minded person's view when it's in favor of your product. You just want to get his authorization on the order. Use this technique only when the customer is biased against your product or service.

In all other instances, you want to speak the language favored by your customer in order to build trust and rapport quickly.

Part II
HOW PROSPECTS
WANT TO BE SOLD

6

Winning with
Different Personalities

You are learning easy strategies for getting along better with all people, which makes your interpersonal relations agreeable and tension-free. Pacing builds rapport. Eye movements help you read how people think and how to speak using their information preferences. You are now in a position to deduce your prospect's behavioral preferences. What type of selling behavior will attract, and what will distract? Your skill in reading speech and body language allows you to interpret and draw conclusions about your prospect's motivations and wants. You will know how to conduct yourself over the telephone and when face to face, how to make a presentation, and how to follow up. You can also anticipate potential sales problems and take preventive measures before they happen.

YOU HAVE TWO MINUTES TO MAKE ME LAUGH

Comedians can teach us about the value of pacing and reading an audience. On the Norm Crosby TV show young comedians competed with one another and the clock to make an audience volunteer laugh against his or her will. The spectacle resembles selling, where provoking a laugh is the same as making a sale. How the three comedians approach each volunteer is interesting to watch and hear. One sizes her up and immediately tries to overwhelm with joke after joke, mugging after mugging, until the two-minute buzzer saves her. The second comedian does the opposite. He fits himself to the person, small-talks, and loosens his victim up against her determined resistance. Suddenly he spots an opening and quickly plunges in with an unexpected verbal uppercut just before the two-minute buzzer. The third comedian surprises the most, at times making faces, saying nothing, yet extracting a smile, at other times talking, joking around, then thrusting his comical cape between the shoulder blades of the now helplessly hysterical victim.

Two-minute encounters with comedians may not exactly be the same as a long-term sales relationship; however, it gets the message across, which is that you should assess whom you are dealing with and maintain flexibility, so that you reduce resistance.

THE FOUR BEHAVIOR STYLES

Everybody can be grouped into one of four behavior styles. All styles have strengths and areas in need of strengthening. There is no such thing as a good or bad style. Styles are indicative of tendencies. Outgoing people, for example, do well in their people relationships but may invest less time and energy in being accurate and reliable. Kind and steady people can be anchors of reliability but may find very little enthusiasm for accepting challenges and making goals. Your personal drive and motivation, your flexibility to adapt to different situations, can usually overcome any handicap, provided you want to achieve the goal badly enough.

On the other side of the coin, it is equally true that any strength overused can become a weakness. Consider getting results as opposed to never being satisfied, being decisive as opposed to domineering, being persistent as opposed to being rigid.

The *dominant* style is characteristic of many leaders in industry, sports, and the military. Also called *driver* or *director*, it puts more weight on results and control than on relationships. Among salespeople this style is an advantage in opening new accounts quickly.

Your prospect is dominant when direct, quick, forceful, impatient, self-assured, demanding, decisive, and responsible.

Persons with this style are Lee Iacocca, Harold Geneen, Peter Grace, George C. Patton, Douglas MacArthur, Jimmy Hoffa, Walter Reuther, Ted Koppel, Vince Lombardi, John Madden, and Archie Bunker.

The *influence* style is characteristic of many sales greats, people-oriented leaders, entertainers, and colorful personalities. Also called *expressive* or *inducer,* this style emphasizes accomplishments through people rather than through overcoming obstacles. One source claims that 72 percent of the world's greatest life insurance producers belong to a subcategory of the influence style. Influencers are enjoyable and entertaining and draw people to them.

Your prospect is an influencer when people-oriented, gregarious, optimistic, enthusiastic, self-promoting, persuasive, emotional, and trusting. Typical public figures of that style are John F. Kennedy, Ronald Reagan, Johnny Carson, Jesse Jackson, Mohammed Ali, Bill Cosby, Ed Koch, Billy Martin, F. Lee Bailey, and Fidel Castro.

The *steadiness* style is characterisic of pleasant, low-key salespeople. Also termed *amiable* or *stable,* they are supportive, loyal, and reliable, wear well, are good listeners, and get along with nearly everyone. They service their accounts very well. They like structure and may be slower in getting started on new projects than people with the previous two styles. Their customers tend to be loyal. They are loyal to their own companies. They resist change and setting goals. Because they do good work, they dislike delegating and may not be sufficiently demanding of others.

Your prospect is a steady when exhibiting behavior described as relaxed, amiable, passive, nondemonstrative, deliberate, patient, and self-controlled. Examples are Dwight D. Eisenhower, Gerald Ford, John Glenn, Perry Como, and Edith Bunker.

The *compliant* style is characteristic of detail-minded technical specialists, who sell on the strength of their product knowledge and their ability to size up people and situations. Also known as *analytical* or *conscientious,* they are perfectionists. They have high standards, are diplomatic and sensitive, but may undervalue the importance of persuasive skills and personal relationships in selling.

Your prospect is a compliant when courteous, precise, accurate, evasive, sensitive, critical, and having high-standards. Typical compliants are Henry Kissinger, Neville Chamberlain, Albert Einstein, Jimmy Carter, Guglielmo Marconi, J. D. Salinger, and stereotypes of CPAs, consultants, therapists, and computer programmers.

All of us have at least some dominant, some influencer, some steady, and some compliant in our makeup. Generally, one of the four is predominant and readily detectable most of the time. What if your prospect shifts from one style to another? Take your cue from the prospect and match the behavior, until the full-blown behavior style emerges after a time. Keep the following points in mind when dealing with people who operate with different styles.

With dominants, be to the point, businesslike, and well prepared. Provide information regarding what you can do. Supply the facts and figures and success probabilities. Offer options to choose from. Talk in terms of results. Avoid competing or disagreeing with them nose to nose. They are competitors. Do not tell them what to do. They resent it.

With influencers, take time to establish goodwill and relationships. Be somewhat entertaining. Talk about people and their goals. Be light in your conversation by avoiding too much detail. Share useful ideas they can put into action. Mention prominent customers and provide testimonials. You are wise to share mutual expectations. Maintain a warm and sociable climate.

With steadies, show interest in them by starting with personal comments. Find areas of common interest or background. Talk informally and casually. Draw them out with respect to their goals and how you can help them get there. Recognize their tendency to go slowly and to procrastinate. They are security-minded. Provide specific solutions at a minimum risk.

With compliants, be prepared with specifics, listing pros and cons of your product and service and what you can do. Bring up objections yourself before they do, and answer them if possible. Develop a schedule for how you implement action and use tangible evidence for your claims, supported by guarantees, in preference to testimonials.

How can you train yourself to do a better job of observing your prospects' traits? Recognizing that many people do some of it by intuition, take one set of traits at a time and practice them for a day. If a prospect is relaxed, open, and informal, be likewise. If he or she is stiff, closed off, and formal, match that formality. Soon he or she will show signs of accepting you and being comfortable with you.

"Just how much flexibility do you expect me to have?"

The answer is, "Enough to be on the prospect's wavelength."

"And suppose I can't?"

The answer is, "Do the best you can with what you have and keep on practicing. You'll like yourself for it."

Suppose I'm a live-wire and my customer acts like he or she is space-warped?"

The answer is, "It's easier for a live-wire to slow down than for a person toilet-trained too early to loosen up. All it takes is practice in forebearance."

By building trust and rapport, accessing the prospect's information preference, and responding to behavioral style, you will sell people in the way they want to be sold, not in the way you want to be sold. You will become a sales master. Remember, behavioral style directs you to what to do, while pacing and eye movements show you how to do it. Each helps make the prospect comfortable with you, so that he or she is emotionally and logically ready to allow you to lead and convince him or her. It is not necessary to be liked every time, but it is necessary to gain acceptance and respect.

7

Determining
Your Prospect's
Buying Fingerprints

Instant Replay

How often have you heard, "You can never know enough about a prospect? The more you know about him or her, the easier it is to sell him or her?"

Here is an example. Kaufman and Broad is an international mass producer of residential subdivisions. While we worked with them, they doubled their sales in our area. But until we got the chance, zillions of gallons of water crashed over Niagara Falls. You see, all requests to meet the divisional president were funneled through the sales manager, who, unhappily, was afraid of him. The result: a temporary impasse.

Fortunately, we were made aware of the appointment of a new sales manager, after which things quickly changed for the better. She was not afraid of her boss and, after listening to our presentation, set up an appointment for us with him.

"What kind of guy is he?"

"Oh, he's really a nice man, but he comes across as somewhat gruff and impatient when you first meet him."

"Oh, a hard-shelled softie. Tell me, if you had to sell him our service, how would you do it?"

"Well, if possible, I would try to do it in five minutes and tell him that right up front. Do you think you could do that?"

"I think it's possible."

"Good. I would tell him what it does, where you did it before, and what he can expect from you. Will you have some proof material with you?"

"Yes. We have testimonials and references."

"That'll be fine."

"Wouldn't he want to know how you felt about it?"

"Oh, sure. Do you want me to be there when you make the presentation?"

"Yes. Would you be willing?"

"Yes. I'd love it."

And so we entered the president's office. A brief introduction by her—an expectant stare by him—an "I know you're a busy man, so I'll come right to the point, it'll take five minutes" by me—a wordless nod from him—some questions and statements and testimonials by me—some grunts by him—a cost quote by me—an inquiring look at the sales manager by him. She said she wanted it. That was good enough for him. He bought.

This little scene had all the elements of instant replay in it, except for one. Had he been the one to reveal his buying pattern instead of she, it would have fully qualified. Few of us are blessed with so much insight about a prospect beforehand. We have to learn how to do it on the spot. How would you like to be your own coach for all of your prospects from here on in? All it takes is knowledge, practice, and the skill of *instant replay,* a technique that photographs all of the elements of your prospect's buying pattern.

What do salespeople want to know about their customers? In capsule form, how to approach, sell, and service them— exactly. This is where the instant replay technique comes in. It puts the blueprint of how to do exactly that right in your hands. How? By asking some simple questions and doing some astute listening.

Just as customers have specific behavior styles, they also have buying fingerprints. The instant replay technique helps the sales master discover not only what the customer considers important but also the sequence in which to present the sales points. In plain talk, the salesperson determines how the customer makes his or her decision on a step-by-step basis. For example, the salesperson will ask, "How did you decide to buy your last drill press? What did you look for first? And what next? And then what? And what was it that finally decided you?"

What has the salesperson done here? First, he or she determined the details of the customer's buying strategy. The salesperson did not just ask the customer, "What's important to you?" Most customers really could not tell you exactly. Next, the salesperson fits snugly into the strategy. And, last, he or she replays that strategy for the customer, who finds it comfortable and familiar. Somehow the customer gets the impression that there is rapport between him or her and the salesperson. That's hardly surprising, because it's his or her own strategy after all. That's why the customer likes it. And since it embraces the salesperson's product or service, the customer is quite willing to accept it.

This is one of the little known skills in the repertory of top producers. They learn their customers' exact order of preference and make sure they walk in their footsteps. Otherwise, they'd be like the waiter who brings you the main course followed by dessert and then appetizer and soup. True, you got what you ordered, but it wasn't in the sequence you expected.

Can you learn what a customer wants from a book? No, only the customer can tell you. Listen to his or her buying strategy as if it were his or her telephone number. If you want to get through to him or her, dial the digits in their proper sequence. One reason why many otherwise competent salespeople don't accomplish more is that they present the right information but in the wrong order and with the wrong emphasis.

But there is more. The sales master can, in the process, probe directly for the predominant buying motive, saying, "Interesting to hear you emphasize stability about the XYZ Company. Mind telling me why you consider stability that important to you in that kind of investment?" Now all the salesperson does is listen, and the client will supply him or her with reasons, rational and emotional. The sales master now knows the customer's buying pattern and emotional appeal. What could be more desirable?

Keep in mind that it takes considerable practice to maintain the conversational flavor—the pacing, the bridging, the communication channel. Avoid coming across like an inquisitor, because it creates tension and reduces trust and rapport.

The instant replay can also extract valuable information for your time and territorial management data bank. For instance, asked how he happened to be still dealing with Snake-Eye Bottling Company, the restaurant owner volunteered that he was generally slow to change brands, no matter what. Loyalties were important to him. "If you ever had to make a change," the salesperson queried, "what would you want from your new supplier that your present one doesn't offer?" The owner opened up, disclosing his buying strategy and predominant buying motive. This combination saved many unproductive sales calls later.

Suppose you worked in a stereo store, and a woman came in to look at video recorders. You'd probably engage her in conversation with "Is this you first visit to Quadrophonic Quality Stores?" and pivot into such qualifying questions, "Are you familiar with video recorders?" "Did you have any special unit in mind?" "Is the video recorder for you or someone else?"

You might find it appropriate to have her look at some units on display. It's during this familiarization phase that she and you develop more trust and rapport, allowing you then to pivot into the question, "What kind of TV set will you hook the new video recorder up to? How did you happen to select that particular TV set?" Notice how easily you were able to branch into instant replay? As you draw her out, she will disclose her important buying elements, buying sequence, and the emotional content of each element to you. You can now instantly replay with the video recorder what you learned from the TV set experience. By carefully listening, you can organize that information, so that it fits into her decision-making comfort zone. She'll love it, because it's a familiar feeling. She's at home with it, and you have made it easy for her to buy from you. In fact, instead of having a buyer, you'll have a customer.

Let's say that her first concern was price, then dependability, followed by style of cabinet (visual), and finally what family and neighbors would say (auditory), a point on which she waxes quite enthusiastic.

You now know her four concerns and the sequence in which they came up: price, dependability, style, what others will say. Play back these points in that sequence and then enthusiastically talk about what others will say about her choice. This is the path through the forest. It is the telephone number that allows you to hear, "I'll buy."

Is there rhyme and reason behind this? Yes. Top producers apply instant replay techniques in getting the clues about the customer's buying priorities, according to the latest research findings. This technique is couched on her thinking and buying habits. All this is assuming you are selling her something she needs and that meets her expectations.

ANATOMY OF A MISSED SALE

Often we learn more from our failures than from our successes. Kai Holmberg's experience serves as a good illustration.

In his initial interview with the executive vice-president of a large printing company, Kai learned that low sales volume was an area of concern. The executive vice-president briefed him about specific problems and personally introduced him to the vice-president of sales.

In a subsequent meeting, the V.P. of sales said that good sales training programs don't exist in their industry. He remembered three experiences when they had failed.

"Perhaps," he ventured, "our business is too complex?" Can instant replay help here? Let's see what Kai did.

Kai: "Dick, I understand where you're coming from. In your judgment, what do you feel was lacking in these programs that made them fail?"

Dick: "Our people are old-timers. They laugh when outsiders talk to them. They say nobody understands our business."

Kai: "That's an interesting point, Dick. Can you be a little more specific in what they're talking about?" said Kai.

Dick: "Well, our selling is different. I don't sell the way they teach and I'm not a bad salesman. I'd say you'd have to work with our people in the field and find out what they do wrong that our field sales managers don't catch. And you'd have to learn their language, Kai."

Kai: "That makes sense to me, Dick. We often go out with salespeople. And knowing the buzz words helps us establish credibility with the salespeople in the training sessions."

Dick: "Good. I'd also want some references."

Kai: "No problem there, Dick. Let me give you a couple to start with."

Dick: "OK."

Kai: "What would it take to help you decide?"

Dick: "I would need to know exactly what you're going to do and how you're going to do it."

Kai: "In other words, you want a detailed outline, right?"

Dick: "Right."

Kai: "OK. I'll commit to making a couple of field trips this week with your people, and I'll supply references and a proposal. Meantime, where do you stand about a starting date and the participants who'll attend?"

Dick: "Let's go for Tuesday in two weeks at 8:30 A.M. I have twenty people in mind who'll be there."

As they said goodbye, Dick suddenly said, "I'll have to check our budget; it all depends on the budget."

"Are you saying we are not holding the meeting then?" Kai asked.

"No, no, no," replied Dick. "I can get the money if I want to."

"And do you want to?"

"Yes."

Kai worked with the people in the field, learned the buzz words, supplied the references, and submitted the proposal. When he called back as appointed, he experienced great difficulty in reaching Dick. When they finally connected, Dick said, "I'm sorry that I didn't check the budget earlier. We can't handle it right now."

"Dick, did you call up the references?"

"No, I didn't."

"Did you check out the people with whom I worked in the field?"

"No, I didn't. Like I told you, sales programs don't work well in our industry."

Instant replay always works. When it doesn't, a post-mortem diagnosis will show either that the salesperson missed a signal or that the prospect for his or her own good reasons deliberately misled the salesperson.

Most customers are relatively honest in sales situations and frequently will offer information just for the asking. They will tell you what you need to know. They will tell you how they make purchase decisions, what kind of information they want first, and what they need to hear from you before they make a decision.

As a result of studying champion salespeople, as well as less successful ones, we have a clear understanding of when instant replay works and fails.

The lack of collecting and organizing the needed information in the early stages of the interview can be disastrous. Top producers ask the right questions and listen well. Less successful people fail to ask the right questions or don't ask enough. Or they may not listen well. They tend to be rigid and lock themselves in. For example, Bud Greenfield's customer liked the safety feature of a revenue bond, leading Bud to concentrate on that single issue to the detriment of other factors such as rate of return, maturity date, and discount. Bud had locked himself into a mind-set. Make certain you do as top producers do, and get a full picture of everything that is important.

Remember that when you pose instant replay questions you involve your customer to the fullest. Lead him or her gently from point to point, so as to give him or her time to reflect on purchasing habits. Global questions, such as asking outright what was most important to him or her tend to be overwhelming and confusing. They might irritate. Have the customer talk about the details of that purchase, instead of some theoretical notion he or she may have about what motivated him or her to buy. Guide the customer to talk about the details of the actual case. You will get more accurate information on his or her sequence. Then you'll be able to play it back with your own product. The only way the customer can resist is to resist his or her own thinking and values, which most customers cannot do.

Take in the whole person—face, hands, body language, and emotional expressions. Look for emotional reactions expressed in slight changes in body language. They gauge the relative strength of each component in his or her buying habit.

Norm Goodman, a door wall distributor, expanded his market by building Door–Wall Patios. He met with his new prospects, the Haywoods. Noticing a large outdoor deck, he proceeded as follows:

> *Norm:* Now, I'd call that an interesting deck. Three levels— unusual. I like the planks on the diagonal. Really an imaginative design.
>
> *Mr. Haywood:* Well, thank you. We get a lot of enjoyment from it.
>
> *Norm:* I bet you do. Whoever did this knew what he was doing. How did you happen to choose him?
>
> *Mr. Haywood:* We responded to several ads.
>
> *Norm:* I see. What made you decide to deal with this contractor? What were you looking for?
>
> *Mr. Haywood:* He showed us Polaroid shots of a few installations. Then he made a sketch of what he proposed to do for us. And then he offered to take us to some of his customers, so we could talk to them and check on the workmanship.
>
> *Norm:* That's a good approach. Anything else?
>
> *Mr. Haywood:* Well, price was a consideration, but not the only one. He turned out to be a little higher, but we liked what he offered for the money.
>
> *Norm:* Interesting. What finally decided you in his favor?
>
> *Mr. Haywood:* He made an appointment to come back with his final sketches and give us a starting date. And when he came back, he surprised us—his design was even better.
>
> *Norm.:* No kidding.
>
> *Mr. Haywood:* Yeah, we'd recommend him to anybody.

Norm had his mental tape recorder going. He excused himself for a moment and soon appeared with an album of Polaroid shots of completed jobs. Using chalk, he outlined the proposed patio site on the ground and sketched two roof designs, discussing the pros and cons. The Haywoods favored one. He asked about their time availability and asked for their permission to phone some customers. The Haywoods readily agreed. After they were duly impressed with a couple of installations, he quoted them a specific price and set up an appointment to review the final architectural design. Not surprisingly, he too seemed to have outdone himself on his second call, and the Haywoods eagerly signed the contract. Norm used the deck builder's strategy as his sales map. It was as simple as that.

In this vignette, Norm focused on the element of value added and the Haywoods' strong emotional reaction and played them in their proper sequence. When a customer shows strong emotions such as delight, amusement, or surprise about one component—be it appearance, price, or reliability—you know that this component is especially important. When you stress it later using similar body language or emotion, it will make its positive impact felt. Top salespeople do this as a matter of course, and it works like magic.

The unobtrusive quality of instant replay makes some people fear it is manipulative. They think it can result in customers buying things they don't really want. Experience does not square with this fear. Most people love to buy. They visit showrooms and stores because of their interest in what is on display. People love to buy, unless an unschooled or insensitive salesperson discourages them by his or her lack of professionalism. Customers are not being victimized by sales skills so much as salespeople are victimized by lack of skill.

Most salespeople tend to follow a presentation sequence based on their own experience or what they've been taught. Their assumption is that others buy the way we want them to buy. Unfortunately, this works only part of the time, because it puts the emphasis not on the customer where it belongs, but on the salesperson where it doesn't.

Instant replay techniques are based on selling the customer instead of selling the product. You are responding to the customer's true needs by presenting the information in the sequence that makes the most sense to him or her. Instant replay techniques help you leave your own pattern behind by concentrating on the customer's needs. They give you a readout on how the customer makes a sales decision. For these reasons, the instant replay techniques work. While it takes some practice and coaching to become skillful, it is well worth the time, for this is among the most powerful tools in the arsenal of champion salespeople.

This has been a discussion of some of the finer details about what makes buying patterns work. Less successful salespeople lessen the power of the technique by getting the buying sequence mixed up. Develop the listening habit and note carefully the customer's purchase priorities. Forget about what you think the order should be. The customer's sequence makes the most sense to him or her.

8

Focusing Your Listener's Screen of Interest

TOO MUCH OF A GOOD THING

As the new preacher approached the pulpit for his maiden sermon, he noticed that the chapel was empty except for a lone old-timer sitting in a pew. The preacher wondered where the rest of the congregation was.

"This is harvest time. They're all out in the fields harvesting," the old man said, "I'm not a well man and no longer do any of that kind of work."

The preacher suggested that under the circumstances it would perhaps be better to cancel the sermon, but the old man wouldn't hear of it. So the preacher mounted the pulpit. After a slow start he began to build up steam and enthusiasm to the point where he got so carried away by emotion that he talked much longer than planned, ending on a high note to drive home his final point.

"Well," he finally said, quite overcome and wiping his brow, "what did you think of that?"

The old man sat there in silence. After a while he answered, "I'm just an old farmer and I don't know much from religion. But I'll tell you this. If I had a whole cart of hay when I feed my cows and find me only one, I sure don't dump no whole cart of hay on her. Do you know what you did, preacher?"

"No."

"You dumped the whole load on me."

THE MYSTICAL SEVEN

The question of what and how much to present to the customer, the client, or the patient is a puzzle to the salesperson, the lawyer, and the doctor to this day. Even professional sales presenters, no matter what medium they work in—slide film, video tape, film—fret about this problem. Is there a formula of some kind to tell you when your customer gets just the right kind of information menu—enough to leave him or her with a good feeling but not so much as to give him or her indigestion or leave him or her hungry? Could you use that formula to anticipate what questions to ask, what points to make, and what objections to prepare for?

Experience shows that to the human mind there is something peculiarly satisfying about seven pieces of information. Seven questions, seven benefits, seven anything defines the optimal attention span for most people, regardless of education or intelligence. Is it coincidental that we talk of the Seven Wonders of the Ancient World, the seven fat years and the seven lean years in the Bible, the seven days of the week, the seven primary notes on the musical scale, the seven close friends in our lifetime, and the seven subordinates who represent the ideal span of control for their manager?

Perhaps of all examples the seven-year itch says it best of all, because it cautions all husbands and wives that after seven years of married bliss the tapeworm of boredom may wiggle in and sap the marriage dry.

What do the top sales producers teach us here? They are experts at capturing and holding their customers' interest—nay, fascination—and they do it quickly and easily.

Jerry Bresser of the Bresser Conferences on Real Estate Sales trains his participants to say the following, here paraphrased:

> "Mrs. Long, there are seven good reasons why you'll benefit by having me represent you to sell your home. What you want is:
> The *most* money you can get,
> as *quickly* as you can get it,
> and with the *fewest* problems possible.
> Isn't that right?"

After this introduction, Jerry lists seven advantages for dealing with him.

In just 15 seconds, with this opening statement, Jerry captures the prospect's complete attention and makes her want to know how he is going to fill in each one of the seven lines on her screen of interest.

She responds, "That's right. Won't you come in and tell me about it?" Incidentally, did you catch all of the general pacing statements, which are impossible to disagree with?

What do average producers do instead? They aren't prepared as well and try to wing it. They fail to pace effectively and don't earn the customer's trust. Noticing their failure to make the expected impact, they try harder. They offer more talk and more information in the hope that more is better. More is not better. More is less in our overcommunicated society. The expression, "If you can't convince them, confuse them," no longer works well, if it ever did.

Like a movie screen, your customers' interests have limited dimensions. When you project too much information, some of it spills over onto the curtains and the chair tops and the walls, and gets lost in the room. Nobody pays attention to it, and you have wasted valuable information.

What if you offered too little information? Now you have another problem. Your presentation is anemic. There are too many empty white spaces on that big screen. The customer looks at these spots, sees only sheer nothingness, gets bored, and daydreams to fill up the gaps.

More makes the customer suffer from information overload, dissipating his or her concentration, diverting his or her attention, and draining his or her interest. *Less* leaves the customer dissatisfied and wondering about your uninteresting proposition and why people do business with you. In either instance, you failed to reach the customer.

Can you tell, as a salesperson, whether you're losing the customer's interest? Yes. Customers flash their little signals as if they were so many lightning bugs. Here is how you can tell: they haven't said one word in the last ten minutes; they keep knitting their brows; they squirm in their seats a lot; they sigh; their eyes get smaller and their eyelids heavier; and the truly fatigued close their eyes altogether, then, startled, pull themselves up abruptly and apologize. And that's not all. The customer is not always the only victim. I know an above average sales producer who has on occasion lulled his customer so effectively that the customer took charge and talked the ears off the salesman to the point where he fell asleep. It's happened more than once.

The *screen of interest* works because that's how your mind is wired. It works because it offers just the right amount of information in the way the customer finds easy to absorb, digest, and act upon. It works because it provides the presenter with the opportunity to gauge the customer's attraction for each one of the seven elements and ultimately discloses the essence of all selling, which is discovering the primary buying motive or buying nerve.

Find the customer's buying nerve with consistency, and you are soaring in the rarefied atmosphere of the eagles. A skilled salesperson plays tour conductor to the customer's tourist by guiding what the customer pays attention to. He or she does so by being in charge of seven variables: emphasis, size, speed, number, clarity, detail, and completeness.

What do you emphasize and prioritize on the screen? What do you lead and end with? What's the theme? How do you vary the size of each piece of information? Are they all alike, or are one or two crowding out the lesser ones? Do you control the speed at which each element is shown? One at a time slowly, or altogether first and in detail later? Do you control the sharpness and completeness of each image? Do you describe each piece in detail or highlight some point and allow the customer to use his imagination otherwise?

Are we saying that once again we had seven examples, which just happened to come up as natural as the roll of dice? Of course not. We distilled many variables to our comfort level of seven. People prefer it that way most of the time. There are individual differences in people in respect to how well they absorb information, of course. Even Albert Einstein had a limited screen of interest, demonstrating that it applies to us all regardless of brain power, memory capacity, or thinking speed. These differences depend somewhat on our abilities and familiarity with the subject. A computer specialist would be expected to absorb more new information about a central processing unit than a rank beginner, because the specialist can easily relate new input to what he or she already knows. He or she hangs new pieces of information on the mental hooks created in his or her mind before. This being so, it's a good idea to describe the screen of interest as "seven plus or minus two."

We are ready now to test the screen of interest concept in the theater of your mind. Make believe, if you will, that you're a film director showing your latest creation to the film's producer, who is your boss. The producer had arranged for all of the financing and now has the job of marketing the film. Since he's the guy who pays you, you want him to be pleased and enthused with your product.

Let's say the film is supposed to sell a new kind of beer and has to make its point in 15 minutes flat. What will you feature on the screen, in what way, and why? You have a large reservoir of ideas to choose from. What market segment do you want to influence? What are your target audience's present drinking habits and preferences? Do they tend to respond favorably to the beer's characteristics of taste, aroma, color, after-taste, lightness? Would they prefer knowing about quality ingredients like barley, rice, and hops, and the source of the water? Would slow aging or filtration or short pasteurization impress them? How about the name, the design of the bottle or can, and the label? Would you consider having the beer displayed against a background of competitive sports like football, or unusual sports like hang gliding, or have it framed against a prestige milieu like an opera bar? Would young or old, men or women be part of the screen? Would you go for comparison taste tests by amateurs who are unaware that their taste buds are influenced by the first swallow of beer? The challenge is to select the significant seven from the trivial two dozen or more. You'll agree it's no small task.

Just think what a tough job producing a TV commercial must be when you can only single out one concept in 30 and then gamble hundreds of thousands of dollars on that one. As salespeople, we at least have the advantage of presenting several of the most likely options and monitoring how our customers react to every one of them.

Here is just one approach of how it can work in practice. Take a sheet of paper and draw seven two-inch lines horizontally, one below the other, being sure that the customer can easily track what you're doing. Now begin developing your interest step by saying:

> "In thinking about the most important factors that go into _____, most executives single out the following six items. First, A, second B,...sixth...F. Since you may like them in some respects yet different in others, what factor(s) do you think ought to be added? Thank you. Any others of significance that should be included? OK. In your experience, how would you rank these factors in in their order of importance? Thank you. In naming the most important, what in your opinion makes it so important to you? The second? The third? If you had the time, what would it mean to you? To your company? Finally, if you could have it, when would you want it?"

When the customer is willing to share his or her preferences with you, he or she will usually lead the conversation by telling you what to fill in. That's the best beginning in filling in the screen of interest.

Most customers tend to know two to four important items already, and it's important to ask them which one is most important and then to fill in the other three to five items he or she has left out.

Experience seems to show that it is useful to help the customer to distill in his or her own mind the top three items that would motivate him or her to buy. Some customers tend to be coy or cautious and hold back when it comes to filling in the interest screen. Here it is wise for the salesperson to suggest four or five items in sequence and to obtain feedback from them regarding significant ideas that ought to go on the screen of interest. When this is done in an atmosphere of pacing, the customer will involve himself or herself more fully. Ideally, the more the customer talks on the issue at hand—which is not the same as time-wasting conversation—the more the salesperson is in control of the interview.

THE LADDER OF EXPECTATION

For a second example, let's discuss a presentation technique used by dentists when helping their patients to upgrade their dental IQs. Here, as well as in the previous illustration, the patient's or customer's screen of interest can be rendered on a sheet of paper, which engages both his or her senses of seeing and hearing. The dentist would draw a horizontal line across the middle of the sheet and draw four large rectangles, one below the other, two above and two below the midline. Writing the word "Emergency" in the lowest rectangle and "Repair" in the one above, he or she would put "Maintenance" in the one above the midline and "Cosmetic" in the top box. The dentist now had five reference points (when you include the midline) and explains briefly his or her definition for each of the five terms—what do emergency, repair, midline, maintenance, and cosmetic mean in terms of the patient's point of reference? Once satisfied that the patient clearly understood, the dentist asked her to identify where she thought she stood on the Dental IQ Ladder and where she wished to be a year or two later. Now the dentist can sit down and help the patient plan the steps to take and how to make the new goal affordable.

Sometimes a customer believes something is important when it may not realistically be, even from his or her point of view. Maybe the customer thinks your product or your company has special advantages, but you know it is common in the industry. You may decide to thank the customer for his or her comments and then enlarge on what makes you unusual. In the rare instance when you take a piece of information off your customer's interest screen, you must replace it with another one. If you don't, your customer will feel that something is missing or something doesn't fit.

You're the calling officer of a large metropolitan bank soliciting large corporate accounts. The vice-president of finance of a corporation has not been made sufficiently aware of a service that both your bank and your competitors offer. On your second call she tells you that the reason she is seriously considering you is because of that service. You're wise in letting her know that you do indeed offer this service. At that point you also provide her with specific advantages about you, which the other bank is unlikely to match, and explain why they are important to her.

Use of the screen of interest requires that you watch your customer for signals about how he or she would like his or her interest screen filled. If the customer comes in talking fast because he or she thinks fast, you can quickly give all seven pieces of information. If the customer wants to focus in slowly on one thing at a time, let him or her set the pace. If he or she asks to see things on his or her interest screen in great clarity and detail, accommodate this. If the customer dislikes facts and details but prefers generalities, speak his or her language and pace his or her mood.

WHAT IF IT DOESN'T WORK?

In some industries, like housing, computers, stereo equipment, machine tools, stock brokerage, or insurance, experienced customers invest a great deal of time in comparison shopping. They may be well versed in the details and will let you know how much they know about the subject. Their message is, "You're not going to put one over on me," or, "See how smart I am." You're pacing them, you're having them in a repeated yes-set, and you're applying the screen of interest principle. Somehow you're not succeeding; you're not making progress. What do you do? You shift gears, you change direction, you try something else—you pace the customer.

Some customers are practiced at setting you up to overwhelm them and to bore them. They ask you quickly for all sorts of information they don't want or need or even understand. When you play their game and flash everything on their interest screen at once—boom!—you've blown it. They are overwhelmed or bored, and leave. What went wrong? You failed to qualify them. You failed to present your answers slowly and in detail, and to confirm that each point is truly significant to them. You failed to ask opinion questions.

As you know, customers are often mixed up and confused. If you are dealing with one who has been shopping and still has not made up his or her mind, chances are he or she has tricked other salespeople into incorrectly projecting things onto his or her screen of interest. This customer has probably not done this intentionally.

Listen to what he or she asks you for. Recognize that other salespeople responded to the requests and probably spent a lot of time doing so. Briefly present the information the customer needs as a matter of courtesy; then move on to fill his or her interest screen with other items that may really make a difference.

Customer: "I'd like a Bimini beige Cadillac Coupe de Ville with the following options: A, B, C, D, E, F. How much?"

Salesperson: "Is this your first Cadillac?"

Customer: "No."

Salesperson: "How often do you buy a new car?"

Customer: "Every two years."

Salesperson: "How many miles do you put on it?"

Customer: "About 23,000 a year."

Salesperson: "Do you generally trade it in, or do you sell it yourself?"

Customer: "Sell it myself."

Salesperson: "In addition to the Bimini beige, what other colors would you seriously consider?"

Customer: "None."

Salesperson: "Let's take a walk. To get a Bimini beige car with all your features will take two weeks. I'm going to show you two other colors that you may like even better. Let's try them on for size."

You show him the first car, and he doesn't like it. You show him the second car, and he may consider it and asks how much it is.

Salesperson: "In addition to what you want, this car has cruise control in it. Are you familiar with cruise control?"

Customer: "Yes."

Salesperson: "Do you like it?"

Customer: "Yes."

Salesperson: "Tell you what. Would you get this car today if you got very special consideration?"

WHEN IT WORKS—WHEN IT DOESN'T WORK

The screen of interest principles work well, so long as they are skillfully used. All human beings prefer things simple and interesting.

Sales professionals selling highly complex products or services face a special dilemma. Their products or services have many more than seven features or details. How do you use the screen of interest principles under these circumstances?

First, of course, you can talk about more than seven of your product's features, but be sure to pictorially or verbally underline the most important aspects, so that these will stay in your customer's attention. You can verbally underline by speaking these words more forcefully, more slowly, with greater emphasis, and by making direct eye contact with the customer to give these words greater impact.

Or, if you have to talk about more than seven aspects of your product, do so in an orderly, professional way, using lots of yes-set questions, so that you and your customer are in step. Group all of the related features together, and talk about them in groups. Do everything you can to keep it simple and make it interesting.

Finally, evaluate your own need to talk about more than seven aspects of your product to that customer. Chances are he or she already knows quite a few things about the product. Don't overwhelm his or her screen of interest with unnecessary details.

Joe Girard, the most successful car salesman in the world, is listed in the *Guinness Book of World Records*. He says, "Most salesmen bore a guy to death when they start to talk about the technical details of a car." He actually refuses to give technical details on cars. If the customer insists, he says, "Look, Mr. Jones, I don't know from gear ratios. If you really want me to find out for you, I could ask somebody in the back to explain all that." He fills the customer's screen of interest with his friendship and caring attitude, with discussions on beauty and styling, and with the social reasons why people want to own new cars.

Remember that the interest screen also applies to you. You may be overwhelming yourself with unnecessary details about your work, which may satisfy your need to be perfect but detracts from the importance of getting on with things. This could lead to excessive stress or burnout. Or you may be boring yourself with your work, because you take too simplistic a view of it all. There are probably only about seven important components to your work. Isn't that reassuring? You don't have to worry about everything in the world.

When you find work boring, you are probably focusing on just one or two aspects of what you do. Whether it is writing an order, telephone prospecting, or repacking equipment, you need to broaden your outlook and fill up those other parts of your screen of interest.

SUMMARY

The screen of interest technique is a multipurpose sales tool that combines important psychological and pragmatic advantages in one format. It takes into account the natural attention span of the customer. It provides the structure necessary to cover the salient points in the sales interview while allowing for the customer's special requirements as they surface in the interview. It helps buyers and sellers alike to help each other in focusing on items of importance or those requiring further discussion. It lends itself to visual, auditory, and action-type presentations. Its structure is applicable to formulating essential questions, interest steps, presentation steps, and possible objections. It represents the "keep it simple, make it interesting" concept.

PART III
SALES LOGIC

9

Utilizing
Bridging Techniques
for Leading People

Bridging is to the ears what motion pictures are to the eyes. When you watch a motion picture, you are really seeing a sequence of still pictures following one another smoothly and rapidly to give you the illusion of continuous motion.When a salesperson speaks in the seeing language and imperceptibly shifts to the hearing or action–feeling–movement language, he or she is using bridging techniques. To the listener, bridging is effortless and elegant. It's free from tension and pressure. Let's try a bridging example on for size.

PRODUCT OF THE YEAR

The 1982 Michigan Product of the Year is a see-through putter, which promises "no more three-putts." Let's pretend you visit a pro shop and pull this new invention off the rack and a salesperson says to you, "Dynamite putter. Getting a lot of attention. It'll take ten strokes off your game. Great invention. See for yourself. Only $69.95."

You may buy that putter on the spot, if $69.95 is within your impulse buying range, or if you three-putt a lot, or for a conversation piece, or as a gift for a good customer. Many golfers would examine it, agree it's a clever invention, and put it back, for any number of reasons. But unless they had spoken to a well-trained salesperson, they might never know what they'd be missing.

How might a sales professional have handled this?

Salesperson: "You are looking at a very interesting putter."
  Customer: "How is it different?"
Salesperson: "Here, let me show you. See the sight in the clubhead? It helps you line up the putter to the cup and the ball." (visual.)
  Customer: "Hm."
Salesperson: "Do you see how it works?" (Bridging to feeling–action.)
  Customer: "Yes."
Salesperson: "How is your putting game?"
  Customer: "I could use some help in that department."
Salesperson: "Here, why don't you get the feel of it?" (Feeling–action.)
  Customer: "OK."
Salesperson: "Feel all right?" (Feeling–action.)
  Customer: "Sure does."
Salesperson: "Some of my best customers have come back and told me they are really pleased. (Bridging to auditory.) It's become a conversation piece around here, and it's been getting a lot of word-of-mouth advertising. You know golfers. They like to talk about their game, and this gives them plenty to talk about, including me. I use it, too, and I can tell you it's shaved a half a dozen putts off my game. I call that exciting."
  Customer: "Sure is. What's the damage?"
Salesperson: "Look at it as an investment in your game and as a conversation piece. (Auditory.) When you play for $1 a hole, it'll pay for itself in two to four weekends. It's only $69.95."
  Customer: "All right. Sounds like fun. I'll take it." (Auditory.)

What did the salesperson do here? He began by pacing the visual aspects of the customer by what he observed about him and what was undeniably true: "You are looking at a very interesting putter." "See the sight..." "It helps you line up..."

Then he spanned from visual to action–feeling–movement with "Do you see how it works?" and continues with "How is your putting game?" "Why don't you get the feel..." "Feel all right?" Once again, he bridges from the action–feeling–movement channel to the hearing channel with "...Customers have come back and told me..." and reinforces that channel using "It's become a conversation piece" and "a lot of word-of-mouth advertising," "like to talk about," "I can tell you." Intuitively or because of heightened awareness, the salesperson recognized his customer as auditory, and when the customer said, "Sounds like fun," he had a double confirmation—that comment and the fact that the customer handed him $69.95 plus tax.

SMOOTH TRANSITIONS

Bridging is the linking, the flowing, the smooth transition from one communication channel to another. It allows you to lead your customers in a comfortable, almost imperceptible way, in keeping with their natural thought patterns. There is nothing erratic or jarring about it, and people feel good because it's done in a completely conversational manner. They are not aware that you are selling.

HOW BRIDGING WORKS

Bridging techniques work by gently refocusing the customer's attention. They are low-key and undetectable. As seen in the above example, the salesperson could have just said "Getting a lot of attention. It'll take ten strokes off your game," and not made the sale. In bridging, he first starts with the customer's present focus of attention—he was examining the putter—and then paces that focus, and by doing so he guarantees that he develops good feelings of trust and rapport. Later he moves from seeing to action–feeling and ultimately to hearing, because the customer responded best to that channel. Contrast this with a salesperson who tells a customer, "Takes ten strokes off your game. Only $69.95." He is leaving too much for the customer to do—and most customers won't bother. True, he's pacing the action–feeling of "ten strokes off your game," but he fails to tune in sufficiently on the customer as a person. Bridging techniques allow you to move the customer from one focus to another, to watch for his or her reaction and response and to be in tune.

BRIDGING IS THE HEARTBEAT OF SEDUCTION

Verbal seduction is a lost art. In today's society, people are forward and direct, permissive and impatient. They rely largely on visual seduction. They go to great lengths making themselves look like Venus or Adonis. Go to a beach and observe bikinis. Or look at their sports cars, convertibles and other driving machines. These people invest heavily in visual selling.

Seduction, another term for superb salesmanship, comes in many forms of which the visual, verbal and physical are the most frequently used. Remember, you are selling, but you avoid signaling your motive if you want to enter the professional ranks. Got it? Play it straight, and play it cool.

What's the first thing you do? You pace things around you that are observable, you pace generalities, you pace body language and speech, all to promote quick trust and rapport, the same as in regular selling. You might pace how you are enjoying yourself, or how you are a little shy when meeting strangers, if that reflects the other person's style also. Only after you have established a good foundation in your interpersonal relationships are you ready to saunter from the topic and lead into other topics.

The second thing you do is to lead the conversation by bridging into other communication channels and topics, taking note of which of the three registers best upon your listener. You will be talking to an interested audience of one, you hope, but there is no guarantee that others won't want to join the conversation.

What will you have accomplished? You will have made a hit. You established trust and rapport, you spoke their language, and in a manner of speaking you have sold yourself.

HOW DON MASSEY SOLD A CADILLAC TO A NONPROSPECT

Ed Ferguson (not his real name) had an appointment to offer a service to Don Massey, a Cadillac dealer in Plymouth, Michigan. Their business completed, Don casually engaged him in conversation, using questions and bridging techniques. Let's follow Don Massey in an example of selling at its best.

Massey: Where is home for you, Ed?

Ferguson: I live over in Rochester.

Massey: I have been there. Pretty town. How did you get here, Ed?

Ferguson: I took I-75 and M-14.

Massey: That M-14 is great. It's a fast track and the most direct route for you. And it's done a lot for our town.

Ferguson: Yeah, it saves a lot of time, and I like the drive.

Massey: I do, too. What kind of car do you drive, Ed?

Ferguson: Cadillac.

Massey: Glad to hear it. Do you like it?

Ferguson: Love it, Don.

Massey: I'm interested. What made you pick Cadillac?

Ferguson: Well, it's a prestige car...

Massey: Un huh. Anything else?

Ferguson: I also like the way it looks...and I got a good deal on it.

Massey: Good. How long have you had it?

Ferguson: Oh, a little over a year.

Massey: Uh huh. What kind of condition is it in?

Ferguson: Oh, it's in good condition, considering the miles I put on.

Massey: What's the mileage so far, Ed?

Ferguson: Around 30,000.

Massey: Color?

Ferguson: Bimini beige.

Massey: Bimini beige. Interesting color. Let's go see it. OK?

Ferguson: What for, Don? You know what it looks like.

Massey: Yes, I know what it looks like, Ed. But we don't see that many here. What do you say we take a look and see what condition it's in, OK?

(Massey starts out the door, Ferguson in tow. He circles the car like a boxer, kicks the tires, and silently walks back to the office.)

Good-looking car. You seem to take good care of it.

Ferguson: Thanks, Don. I try.

Massey: I can see that...but something is puzzling me, Ed.

Ferguson: Puzzling you? What's that?

Massey: Didn't you tell me you chose Cadillac because it's a prestige car and because of its looks?

Ferguson: Right.

Massey: Then how come you aren't seen in the latest model, Ed?

Ferguson: Money.

Massey: Sounds familiar. Money stops a lot of people, Ed. What they fail to consider is whether it's an expense or an investment in their business. There is a big diffference, Ed, right?

Ferguson: I'm not so sure, Don. A new car costs money, no matter what you call it.

Massey: That depends on how you look at it, Ed. How often do your clients see you in your car?

Ferguson: A few times a week, I guess.

Massey: That's what I thought. Do you think some of them notice when you drive a new car and when you don't, Ed?

Ferguson: I suppose some of them do.

Massey: What do you think goes through their minds when they see you in a new Cadillac?

Ferguson: What are you driving at?

Massey: What I'm driving at is the image you project to them with a new car. Isn't it true that people do businesss with you because of how they see you and how successful you appear to them?

Ferguson: (Nods.)

Massey: Isn' t that why you are driving a Cadillac in the first place?

Ferguson: That's true, Don. But a year-old car gets me by, too.

Massey: It may get you by, but you won't know when it doesn't. Just ask yourself, are you being consistent with the rest of your appearance? Why do you wear custom-tailored suits and shirts? Why do you wear that watch? Let me tell you why. For the same reason you prefer a Cadillac. To project that image of success. Will you agree with me that that's what a new Cadillac will give you that your present car can't—that image of success?

Ferguson: Well, perhaps.

Massey: Let me make it real easy for you. All you need to ask yourself is, "What would it take to own a new Cadillac?" That sound fair to you?

Ferguson: Yeah. That's a good approach. All right, what if I traded mine in. How much would it take?

Massey: All right, let's see how good a guesser you are, and maybe I'll surprise you.

Ferguson: $5000.

Massey: You're in the ball park. Let's make that $4000, OK? For $4,000, you get to own a new Cadillac, which is better looking, makes a better impression on your clients, and best of all is a morale booster for you. That right?

Ferguson: Yes. But it also costs $4000 more, Don.

Massey: You're right there. It's $4000 more, but it can bring you $20,000 or $30,000 additional business.

Ferguson: What do you mean, Don?

Massey: Suppose I could show you that that's a true statement. What would you say to that?

Ferguson: I'd say you'd have my undivided attention.

Massey: It's simple. All you do is figure out how many clients or deals you need to make up for the $4000 difference. My guess is you probably need only one or two. Am I wrong?

Ferguson: No...no, you're on target.

Massey: My second guess is there are at least 50 clients who know you drive a new Cadillac every year, and if only 10 percent are influenced by that, you've made an extra $20,000 or $30,000.

Ferguson: Good point.

Massey: Now I'm going to tell you something that will make you feel even better. Let's take it one by one, OK?

Ferguson: OK.

Massey: A car in your model today is $1500 more than when you bought yours. If you'll keep it in as good condition as this one, how much more do you think you'll get for it after a year, Ed?

Ferguson: No idea, Don.

Massey: At least $1000 or better. Will you remember that figure, Ed?

Ferguson: OK.

Massey: Then you've got depreciation...you've got tax savings...you won't need new tires...no repair costs because it's under warranty. How much do you think that will save you, Ed?

Ferguson: Another thousand?

Massey: At least. Depends on your income, of course. Altogether, you can take $2000 or more off the $4000. We're talking about less than $40 a week. Sound good?

Ferguson: I'm still listening, Don.

Massey: And there is something else that's even more important, Ed.

Ferguson: What's that?

Massey: A new car acts like a sales manager for you. It gives you built-in motivation, a can-do spirit, and therefore gets you to work smarter and harder than you ever had to before. You have to think more, be more innovative, grow more, do a better job, and have a better attitude. That's why the new car is good for you. That's why you need it. Make sense to you?

Ferguson: (Nods.)

Massey: I want you to go home tonight and surprise your wife with your new car. What color does she like, Ed?

Ferguson: I have no idea.

Massey: Here is the telephone. Call her.

Ferguson: No, I can guess. I'll pick the color.

Massey: OK. Let's go pick one.

Ed Ferguson drove home that night in a new Cadillac. It was the last thing he would have thought of when he got up that morning. Years later I told this story to the regional manager, and as the story unfolded his face broke out in a big grin.

"Why are you smiling like that?" I asked.

"Because Don Massey is just about the best salesman the division ever had. He has the unique honor of being the first man ever to make the Cadillac Hall of Fame."

If you tried to follow traditional sales patterns of approach, interest, presentation, desire, and close, you'd experience a lot of difficulty in structuring this kind of verbal exchange. What's more, it all seems so easy and so natural that to untrained eyes and ears it's almost unimpressive. Actually it is loaded with powerful persuasion techniques, whose value has not really been recognized. Great salespeople like Don Massey have been using them intuitively all along.

THE THREE RULES OF BRIDGING

Rule 1—Always Start with Your Customer's Present Focus of Attention

You match the customer's focus of attention, and by doing so you guarantee that you will develop more good feelings and trust. In contrast, a salesperson who simply tells the customer to do something does not show respect for that customer's current focus. It's too abrupt. The salesperson is moving the customer without adequate preparation, which often results in hesitation, doubt, and feeling pressured. The customer hasn't been properly led into the right mood. Bridging techniques are the heart of seduction.

Rule 2—Move Smoothly from One Sensory Focus to Another

If the customer is fixated on the way your product sounds or should sound, move his or her attention to the way it looks. You can persuasively go from the way it feels to the way it sounds, or any other combination. In other words, you can go from any sensory focus of attention (the way it looks, sounds, or feels) to any other sensory focus.

Rule 3—Link One Feature or Advantage to Another One

Suppose you encounter a price shopper. Many people have a much better emotional understanding of money than of the value of a home, a car, a computer, a lawn mower, or an antenna. They lack the experience, and it's up to the salesperson to help them understand and appreciate the value in terms of money or other emotional appeals, such as fun, health, respect, growth, friendship, safety, or service. When your price shopper asks, "How much?" use your powers of observation, and after answering the question first, bridge into other communication channels to cover untapped areas of interest.

THE FOUR APPLICATIONS OF BRIDGING

Develop a Fuller Appreciation of Your Product or Service

If your customer is highly visual, he or she may rave about a house you've shown. The customer has probably talked with other salespeople about the same thing—the beauty of houses he or she was shown. To get the customer to make a purchase decision, get him or her to develop a fuller appreciation of all of the features and benefits of your house. You do this with questions or demonstrations. Be careful not to cut off or minimize the customer's appreciation of the visual aspects. You want to amplify that visual aspect that he or she likes so much as your golden gateway.

Defuse Resistance and Objections and Rekindle Interest

If you encounter resistance or lack of interest in any feature under discussion, go back to the original focus of attention. The customer will immediately perk up, allowing you to bridge back to the new area later on. Remember, the fuller an appreciation of your product a customer has, the more irresistible and compelling it will become.

Work with Rigid or Prejudiced People

Bridging techniques work especially well with people who are stuck in rigid thought patterns or limited ways of experiencing their world. Someone said, "A rut is a grave with the ends kicked out." If your customer is totally obsessed with the way your product looks, or with a little scratch on the paint, there is no need to try to change his or her mind directly. You can acknowledge the current focus of attention and then bridge into a new focus of attention.

Work with Indecisive Customers

Bridging techniques also work remarkably well with customers who can't make up their minds. I am sure you have had customers like this. They have been to all kinds of showrooms and looked at everyone's products. They are really serious about buying, but they just can't make a decision. These people are perfect candidates for bridging.

Bridging is an all-purpose persuasion tool, because you will speak the other person's language. Whether you are in sales or not, it will add measurably to your conversational skills, and once you master it you will notice that people tend to follow your recommendations and leadership more than ever before.

10

Employing the Modern Persuasion Strategies of Mental Hinges and Mental Erasers

MENTAL HINGES—A SALES LOGIC TECHNIQUE

As a sales professional you are undoubtedly familiar with the difference between order taking and selling. Some products are so new or unique that they have no competition. Some sales territories lack competition. In some cases the price is so low or the advertising so persuasive that customers flock in to take it out of your hands. All of these are examples of order taking, not selling. As long as the customer feels he or she can trust you and your company, that customer will buy. He or she enters, mind already made up, and all you do is take the order.

Selling, on the other hand, involves influencing and motivating the customer to action. It is still important to have the customer respect and trust you, but this is usually not enough to make a successful sale.

The selling or influencing skills of the master salesperson are based upon particular ways in which words are used to guide the thoughts and emotions of customers. These influencing skills, here called *mental hinges,* work by connecting an undeniably true statement with whatever the salesperson wants the customer to experience next. They are the power-packed little words that top sales producers use with great frequency and others don't use nearly enough. Mental hinges can be placed on a scale ranging from weakest to strongest:

And Or	As While	Make Cause
But	During Since	Force Require

Weakest		Strongest

The mental hinges *and, or,* and *but* are weakest, because they merely suggest an association of two events being hinged together. For example, "You are standing here looking at this microcomputer, *and* you can picture how it can increase the efficiency of your office." The mental hinges *make, cause, force,* and *require* are the strongest, because they state a necessary connection between the two events. "Just seeing the styling of this car will *make* you want to buy it." There are times when you want to use the weaker forms and times when you want to use the stronger ones. These are explained later.

Since the first part of the mental hinge has to be true, the customer must accept it. "You are standing here looking at this microcomputer..." This obvious statement is then linked to the leading part of the sentence. "...And you can picture how it can increase the efficiency of your office." In this example, the mental hinge *and* links the first statement to a second statement that leads the customer to think about improved office efficiency with the computer. Since the customer can't help but accept the first part of the sentence, he or she tends not to question the second part either. The customer swallows it like a pill, because the doctor decided it's good for him or her. Actually, he or she has been led.

Salespeople who know how to use mental hinges never run out of things to say. Anything around you, anything that is observable, any truism, any proverb, anything that qualifies as a pacing statement serves as the first leaf of the hinge to which the salesperson attaches the second leaf in order to open the customer's mind to new ideas, to good feelings, to new experiences, to whatever the salesperson wants to communicate. Mental hinges can be used throughout the sales interaction, from the opening to the close. They are the glue of all conversation and are much easier to listen to than talking as if you were using commas and periods.

Mental hinges work for good reason. We use them continually to think, to imagine, to reason. We see, hear, or sense things, and arrive at cause-and-effect judgments. In our heads we are forever connecting events, whether related or not. Top salespeople know this well. By replaying this process that takes place in our heads, they make it easy for their customers to listen and follow them. They imitate nature, much like comedians and entertainers do when they make everyday observations and connect funny conclusions to them. What could be more natural, more effortless than that? They imitate nature like a photographer using a camera. When the photographer shoots a landscape with tree branches in the foreground and mountains in the background, he or she chooses an infinity setting. When he or she has someone sit for a portrait, the depth of field setting is determined exactly by the distance to the subject.

Do mental hinges work with everyone? Yes, they do. Still, you want to select them with the same good judgment as photographers choose their settings. As was said before, mental hinges vary in their relative precision but not in their relative value. There are occasions when the best influencing technique is a general or weak mental hinge, such as *and* or *but*. On other occasions, a precise or strong mental hinge is called for. Here are some guidelines.

Hint 1

Top sales producers purposely choose weak mental hinges early in the sale. They only suggest an association of two events and are therefore almost impossible to disagree with.

Hint 2

Mental hinges such as *since, as, while,* and *during* are more useful in the middle of the sales interaction, after you have developed some trust and rapport. "As long as you are already in the car, go ahead and start it." Here there is no doubt that the customer is sitting in the car. The mental hinge *as* connects this bit of reality to the leading statement that the customer should start the car.

Hint 3

Top sales producers save the srongest mental hinges for last, for the close. The customer has to trust you and believe in you for these to be as powerful as they can be, or they are wasted. They imply that two things are absolutely connected and that one causes the other. "Putting high-tech entrepreneurs, venture capitalists, and universities together will cause this state to become one of the wealthiest in the nation." Here, the mental hinge *cause* is used. These strong mental hinges can also be effective early in the sales interview when you use them to set up positive expectations for the customer.

I was observing one of the top real estate agents in central Oregon in action. She said to a customer, "Now, I'm not sure I want to show you this last house. It is just a little out of your price range, and it is so beautiful that just looking at it will make you want to buy it." She used the *make* mental hinge to set up a positive expectation in the mind of the customer. He looked forward to a beautiful house, and when he saw it, he fell in love with it and bought it.

Sales Logic

Salespeople can be too logical in their sales presentations. They speak in short, choppy sentences. They don't know how to tie things together. They sound dry, square, and lifeless. In computerese they would be termed "not user friendly." When you listen carefully to top producers, you will hear longer, flowing sentences that tie everything together, even if it doesn't seem related. Label this *sales logic*.

Top sales producers focus on the listener rather than the product. Their best-developed trait is flexibility. They use whatever is happening or whatever is available to make the sale. They have maze brightness, the kind of intelligence that helps you make it in life even if you didn't make it through high school. Don't limit yourself to rigid, old-fashioned logic in making your sales presentations. To enjoy the success of a master salesperson, speak like a master salesperson. Enjoy using mental hinges to make the connections you need to make the sale.

MENTAL ERASERS—ANOTHER SALES LOGIC TECHNIQUE

The billboard along the highway screams, "Incredible—Stu Evans Ford Sells for Less." On a quiet country road another sign reads, "Freshly Laid Eggs." The political poster claims, "Clearly the People's Choice. He has done more for the state than any other elected official." Signs like these are commonplace and talk to us in everyday language.

Stu Evans doesn't tell you what he means by "sells for less." Less compared to whom? Does it apply to all models or only some? On special days or all week? When you analyze it, his outdoor sign really doesn't mean much, but it sounds good.

People get hooked by this type of verbal bait all the time, but they really don't care. The good negotiators among them will really buy their cars for less, as they would at any other dealer. The less motivated will not know the difference anyhow. They will think they got it for less, because that is what the sign said.

In a similar vein, "Freshly Laid Eggs" is not the same as "Eggs Laid Today, Sunday 6/19/85 at 3:00 A.M." "Clearly the People's Choice" will make sense only after the election returns are in, not before. "He has done more for the state than any other elected official" leaves it all to the electorate's interpretation. More of what? Compared to whom? Perhaps he spent more money for the prevention of sun stroke in polar bears or introduced four House bills for the development of a computerized slingshot industry in northern Michigan.

The posters reflect pretty much how we speak. And in general conversation that is usually sufficient. True, you may occasionally get a request to be more explicit. And that's all right—just give them enough and get on with it. Or throw a truism in the questioner's direction, such as "wanting to avoid not seeing the forest for the trees" or "looking at the big picture," and leaving the details for later. Chances are people will want to understand and, because you don't overwhelm or bore them with details, they will like your presentation.

What are Mental Erasers?

Mental erasers are one or two ordinary words that give the impression of being specific and powerful, but on closer inspection really aren't. They're masqueraders. They are an illusion, and that is why they work so well on the listener's mind. They make it possible for your customer to arrive at his or her own personalized meaning of what he or she hears and to put the stamp of his or her interpretation on it. They project power. They instill confidence. Because they sound so absolute, they are reassuring, and it's easy for the customer to make a positive decision. Examples are:

- "Clearly this is your best choice."
- "She obviously likes them."
- "There is no better towel anywhere."

Why an illusion? Look at the three examples once more and ask, what makes it clear? Best choice on what basis? What makes it obvious? Better according to whose standards?

Three Types of Mental Erasers

Type of Eraser	Sample Eraser Words	Information Erased
-ly erasers	clearly, obviously, certainly, definitely	Clear to whom? What makes it obvious?
-er and -est erasers	faster, slower, prettiest, strongest	Compared to what? What makes it so?
less and more, least and most erasers	less expensive, more efficient most valuable, least difficult	Compared to what? What makes it the most or least?

A trained salesperson spots mental erasers the moment a customer intuitively defends himself or herself with them in the close and disarms them with questions preceded by a softening statement.

- "I certainly see/hear/get a feeling of where you are coming from, Ms. Customer. Would you please tell me what you mean by...? (softening statement)

- "Obviously they've got you beat on price." (I am not sure why it is obvious.)
- "Definitely too expensive for you." (Why definitely?)
- "Clearly your current service is better." (Better in what way?)

The potency of mental erasers may come as a surprise to you. Their motivational impact is great, yet the more analytical you are, the less favorably you may initially react to them. They fly in the face of what you were taught in school and college. For example, avoid -*ly* words in compositions as much as possible. With *more* or *less* words, complete the idea as in "Stu Evans Sells All His Fords for Less Than Any Other Downriver Dealer." Or "This is the best jacket as regards tailoring." Clearly, good writing and great selling are different languages, not as much as French and German, but different all the same.

With a little adaptability and flexibility, even a Rhodes Scholar can make it as a salesperson. So there is hope for everyone.

What dynamics account for the power of mental erasers? The power of suggestion. Why then do we respond so willingly? Because they escape detection. Instead they channel your customer's thinking along certain predetermined lines and cause him or her to develop positive expectations about what he or she hears from you. When you tell someone, "This is the finest policy in the industry," everything you say after that will be interpreted as being part of the "finest" (-*est* eraser) group. In a sense, mental erasers are picture frames of words. If you've ever had to choose a frame, you know the different effects you can get with a stainless steel and glass combination compared to one made of carved wood. In the same sense your words frame everything the customer will visualize in his or her mind. That is why the words you use early in your presentation are so important. They frame everything you say later. Mental erasers are frames made by you into which your customer puts his or her picture. That picture, while his or her creation, is based on his or her interpretation of what he or she perceives. That is why the customer likes it and believes in it with conviction. He or she will fill in positive details. Obviously he or she is suggestible.

This skill of tapping into the customer's imagination has been refined to an art form by master salespeople, who employ it far more often than other people. They use it with everyone, even with technical and analytical people. They particularly apply it at the beginning and at the end of a sales interview. They expect to build positive expectations at the outset and want to leave them with positive expectations for the close and for the next meeting.

Why do so many people prefer the story in a book to the film they see later? Why do people believe they see lifelike likenesses in clouds? Why do ink blot tests work? All of them have you see the world according to the dictates of your imagination and your view of the world, and this is very pleasing to you.

Who else uses a lot of mental erasers? Obviously, advertisers, political leaders, self-help authors, religious leaders, financial newsletter writers, even doctors—in short, people with the best of credentials in our society. They do it because it gets the job done. It works. Only occasionally will someone complain that they promise more than they can deliver, even though that may be the fault of that person's own interpretation.

President Ronald Reagan in his September 24, 1981, address to the nation used 17 mental erasers. Can you find them?

> Shortly after taking office, I came before you to map out a four-part plan for national economic recovery: Tax cuts to stimulate more growth and more jobs. I was especially pleased when a bipartisan coalition of Republicans and Democrats enacted the biggest tax cuts and the greatest reduction in federal spending in our nation's history.
>
> Well, that budget...hemorrhaged badly and wound up in a sea of red ink. I have pledged that we shall not stand idly by and see that same thing happen again. When I presented our economic recovery program to Congress, I said we were aiming to cut the deficit steadily to reach a balance by 1984. ...For more and more working Americans, the Social Security tax is already the biggest tax they pay.
>
> I believe there are better solutions. It was never our intention to take this support away from those who truly

need it. ...But, and this is most important, those early retirees would only have to work an additional 20 months to be eligible for the 80 percent payment. ...They deserve better from us.

Notice that two of these persuasive sentences used by the president each contained three mental erasers. After you have identified all of the mental erasers, classify them. See how many are -*ly* erasers, *least* and *most* erasers, and -*er* and -*est* erasers. If you can locate a copy of the president's short speech, you will find he used more than two dozen other mental erasers besides the ones shown here. The president and his speech writers knew the power of mental erasers and used them well.

Difficult Customers

With suspicious customers, you want to combine mental erasers with truisms, statements that are undeniably true and impossible to disagree with. For example, a salesperson in a prestige company like IBM can say, "Obviously nobody gives better service than IBM." The customer's mind will fill in the details about why this is obvious. Or the salesperson could say, "Clearly this is the best software for your needs." This sets up a powerful positive picture in the customer's mind.

In another sense, mental erasers are like vitamins. They work best when used frequently during your presentation. You can't use them just once or twice and then allow yourself to get discouraged when you don't see results immediately.

Some champion salespeople use two or three mental erasers in one sentence. For example, "This is easily the most exciting sports car for the money." "Certainly you and I know that this is the best value of any house in the area." "Obviously this word processor has the greatest appeal to the people who'll use it."

How can you tell when mental erasers are not working or have been overused? Look for your customers reaction as a tip-off. Once he or she asks for a lot of details, oblige. You truly need to know you're overdosing him or her. As soon as the customer seems satisfied, go back to using positive mental erasers. Guide his or her mind in a positive way for a positive outcome, and he or she will fill in positive details.

How They Work

Mental erasers work by simplifying things for the customer in that they involve his or her mind and attention.

Often average salespeople tend to talk too much or recite dry and boring facts about their products or services. All customers, even smart ones, like things simple. Mental erasers allow you to do this and come across like a pro. Joe Girard, the world's most successful car salesman, says, "I don't know from technical knowledge about automobiles. Hell, that's not what they're buying. You'll just scare most of them away when you get into gear ratios and horsepower."

When you tell a customer that an insurance policy will fit his or her needs "perfectly" (*-ly* eraser), his or her imagination will tell him or her what "perfectly" means. When you tell a customer that a contract is "best suited to his or her needs" (*most* eraser), his or her unconscious mind will tell him or her what that means.

When you use mental erasers, you get the customer's mind to fill in the specifics you have left out about what makes the contract "best suited to his or her needs." And the details his or her mind will come up with will be more meaningful than any fact you could ever give. This is a scientific truth. The customer believes what he or she comes up with and therefore is apt to believe you, too, and trust you. This is another way to build good feelings between the two of you.

To most salespeople this spotlight on mental erasers is a stunner at first. Most have never even heard of them before, much less understood their power. Yet their own prospects rub them out with these mental shadows every day of the week.

Recently I worked with an ad salesman of a major metropolitan newspaper, calling on prospects he couldn't shake loose. Here is how one of them responded to "Why don't you deal with us instead of the competition?"

The prospect replied, "I'll tell you why. Your competitor gives me a better deal. You know that. You give me a better deal, and I'll deal with you."

My salesman friend, having made six calls on that man before, shrugged and looked to me as if I were the Lone Ranger.

Me: "Will you help clarify something for me?"

Customer: (Nods.)

Me: "When you say that the other paper gives you a better deal, what do you mean?"

Customer: "They give me a 30 percent discount off the normal rate."

Me: "I see. So what you're saying is that instead of costing you $1000, you only pay $700. Do I have that right?"

Customer: "That's right."

Me: "Aren't you forgetting something, though?"

Customer: "What?"

Me: "According to some of the customers I have met, you get at least a 30 to 50 percent better response from him. (Pointing to my friend.) So let's see what that means in dollars and cents to your business. Are you game to go?"

Customer: "Sure."

Me: "For your $700 with the other paper you get about $7000 worth of business. For $1000 to our friend here, you'll get at least $10,000 in return. In other words, the extra $300 invested in the ad brings you an extra $3000 in business. I bet you guys never looked at it that way, did you?

Customer: "No, I guess we didn't look at it that way."

We got the ad. Notice how the customer first used the mental eraser on us and, as they say in poker, how we called him on it. Notice also how we used our own mental eraser on him and he let it go by. Actually, the return on investment was 10 percent in both situations, but that is not the only yardstick in making a choice, of course.

Can you appreciate now the hidden power of mental erasers when used against you? Do you understand how you can defend against them in the future? And, particularly, can you sense the impact it'll have when you use them with your prospects to get them to think things through completely? Use mental erasers to help your prospects make decisions for you and your product.

11

New Uses for
the Repeated Yes
Technique

As I review my New Year's resolutions, I see that the B Company is again on my list of target accounts. During the past two years I have met six managers there without making significant inroads. The company seems an ideal prospect. It has huge potential for us and is in proximity to our offices. My problem comes in two parts: Find out who the real decision maker is and then get a favorable introduction to him or her. This time I decide to go to the top using the cold call technique. Striding across the lobby to the reception desk, I ask for the chief executive officer.

"Gil Rogers, please."

"Who may I say is calling?"

I give her my name, but no card.

"Do you have a card?"

"It's not handy, Miss Carr. I am sorry. I would like to surprise him."

She smiles, calls upstairs, and then informs me that he is out of town this week.

"Who is the ranking corporate executive who would see me for a few minutes? I need someone at a high level to give me some guidance. It's important."

Miss Carr signals that she understands and begins dialing.

"We are in luck," she reports. "The vice-chairman will be glad to talk to you for a few minutes."

"Thanks for your help. I really appreciate what you have done."

The vice-chairman turns out to be an open and unaffected man, who comes right out and says, "Now tell me what you need, and let's see if I can help."

I thank him and proceed. "Thank you for your help-fulness. Do you mind if I close the door?"

"Not at all." ("Yes, you can close it.")

"Do you mind if I introduce myself first, then tell you what I am about?"

"No. That's fine." ("Yes, proceed.") I quickly thank him, give him some background information, and continue, "What if I told you that we have found a way of dealing with a special plant problem that is of great interest to many heads of operations in your general industry. Do you think your man would be receptive enough to want to listen?"

"I am sure he would," the vice chairman says. (Yes.)

"Sounds promising," I add, reinforcing him.

"Tell me a little more about it."

"Here is what we have learned from our clients. It seems the challenge that operations is currently facing is.... Is that about the way you are finding it?"

"Sure is." (Yes.)

"And what you are indicating is that it is an important enough issue for your operations people to discuss in detail?"

"Oh, absolutely. I think he would want to know. Of course, you understand that any decisions are up to him. I cannot promise you anything."

"I understand. Would I be out of line asking you perhaps to arrange a meeting with him for me? I would be pleased to go over it with him."

"Don't mind at all. Let me see if he is in his office." (Yes.)

The vice-president of operations is out of town. Ray, the vice-chairman, leaves a message and tells him to expect my call. We shake hands heartily for having made progress together. Several days later I call the vice-president of operations. He immediately surprises me with his warm tone, saying, "I have been expecting your call. Ray told me all about you."

It is the beginning of a long and productive relationship, thanks in part to the structured questions, which resulted in the *repeated yes technique.*

Empathy and the will to win are critically important traits for top sales performers.

A great way to create vibes of empathy while maintaining the will to win is by means of the repeated yes technique, a powerful mover of people because of its unique ability to develop feelings of agreement between you and the customer. Done habitually by professional persuaders, the repeated yes feels good to the listener. Top persuaders absorb it more or less by osmosis, and so long as you want to learn from them and apply it to ethical ends, you will benefit from it. And you'll save your voice in the process, because salespeople do not get paid by the word.

What is the repeated yes technique? It's a special way of talking that gets other people to want to say yes to you or agree with you with a nod or an OK. It's ingratiating without being obvious.

Repeated yes's are like so many cables for your communication bridge to the customer. Build a solid structure between you now and for the future. To the customer the repeated yes becomes a mind-set. By agreeing with you with a yea and a yippee, he or she wants to keep on being on your side and rooting for your success. Did you ever shop for furniture or appliances with adult family members and discover that you took sides with the pleasant salesperson over your kin, who became an embarrassment to you? Perhaps the salesperson has simply been repeat-yessing you.

You have a variety of repeat yes structures to choose from. Ben Feldman, the Babe Ruth of selling, would say, "Will you agree with me?" Variations are:

- "Have you found...?"
- "Would it be fair to say...?"
- "Do you sometimes find...?"
- "In your experience...?"

- "Do you ever encounter...?"
- "Does this sound like something you've heard before?"

A second way to structure a yes set is to make a statement and end with "OK?"

- "Watch the dial, OK?"
- "Use regular paper with this copier, OK?"
- "Hold the club like this, OK?"

Notice the softening effect of that OK. Notice how it literally asks for agreement. If you get tired of OK, try "all right?"

A third and similar structure is to say something and follow up with "Do you see?" "Is that all right?" "Any problems?" "Do you follow?"

A fourth way to get a yes is to turn an obvious generalization—some people call it a trite saying—into a question:

- From "Everybody likes a bargain." to "Everybody likes a bargain, don't they?"
- From "Customers expect good service" to "Customers expect good service, don't they?"

Again, listen to how this request for agreement builds people bridges. Here are more:

- "Been a long time, hasn't it?"
- "Don't see much of that any more, do we?"
- "Hot today, isn't it?

A fifth way is to repeat back what the customer says and nod your head in the affirmative.

- "You like it?
- "You're 28?"
- "You're an engineer?"

Notice the suggestiveness of the nod. It's a way to communicate friendliness and acceptance and generates a yes response.

WHEN A NO IS A YES

The English language has certain peculiarities, and one of them is that a no sometimes means yes. You wouldn't want me to confuse you, would you? You say no. Do you then mean you would want me to confuse you? Let's unscramble this mess. You are saying, "Yes, you're right. No, I don't want to be confused." How about these: "You wouldn't want to miss on extra profits, would you?" "No, I wouldn't. (Yes, you're right)." "You don't want to be second best?" "No, I wouldn't. (Yes, you're right)."

BRIDGES TO THE CUSTOMER

Of the few ways to engineer for agreement, the repeated yes technique, which consists of a series of closed questions dispersed in the conversational stream, is the easiest one to follow and practice.

What is the difference between yes sets and pacing? Yes sets are one way of pacing generalizations and observations. Yes sets are used in leading. Yes sets are used for hidden action commands. When you combine yes sets with pacing body language, loudness, and tempo of speech, you reach the customer's head and heart, which is the best way to make a sale.

Jim Alexander was a great salesman and an even greater sales trainer. He'd observe you in action with one customer while quietly fading into the woodwork and then present you with an eight-page report. On its front page he'd write, "Fire Yourself," or a similarly reassuring headline, and while handing it to you he'd tell you to read it just before going to bed. Jim had a lot of talent. People admired his ability to have others want to be in step with him even though they had only just met him. Jim was a practiced yes-setter.

> *Jim:* Mr. Jones, can I ask you a question?
> *Customer:* Sure.
> *Jim:* Just suppose it were possible to obtain savings of $100,000 using a technique that you would be comfortable with. Would you be interested in listening?
> *Customer:* Sure. What are you talking about?
> *Jim:* Will you agree with me that for most of us it is important to raise our quality while getting better results from our resources?
> *Customer:* Of course.
> *Jim:* Would you say that quality improvement is not a sometime thing but an all-the-time thing?
> *Customer:* Yes.

Jim: Is it a fair statement to say that the more people we can get in the boat in working on quality, the better the overall result would tend to be?

Customer: Of course.

Jim: Do you feel that quality is of singular importance in maintaining competitive levels of productivity?

Customer: Yes.

Jim: Can we say that without quality productivity is meaningless today?

Customer: Just about.

Jim: Would your competitive position be more secure if you succeeded in lowering your reject rate and cost while raising your output?

Customer: Yes, of course.

Jim: Latest statistics from quality improvement centers and productivity centers claim that on the average you save 30 percent or more of the cost of operations in service companies and 20 percent of sales in most manufacturing companies. If you saved only half as much, will you agree that would be considerable?

Customer: It certainly would.

Jim: Any reason you could see why you wouldn't want to do something about it as soon as practical?

Customer: None that I know of.

A TOOL FOR LEADING THE CUSTOMER

Take a look at these examples and get the feel of their power to lead:

- "Do me a favor and look at these figures, OK?"
- "Be a buddy and watch that door, OK?"
- "Give us a smile, OK?"

Can you see how the OK can itself become an anchor and how it takes a command and softens it to the point of sounding like a request instead of an order?

The repeated yes technique gets customers to say yes, yes, yes, yes. They even say it out loud and can end up sounding like a tape loop or warped record. They get customers into the yes habit, and when it's time for the close, what could be more natural than to say yes after all that practice?

WHY IT WORKS

The repeated yes technique is a multipurpose sales tool. First it builds positive expectancy in the mind of the customer by furnishing him or her with can-do facts and a will-do spirit. The customer begins to expect the positive, to look for the positive, and to discover the positive. And after finding it, he or she will be more likely to buy, right?

Second, when you get the customer to accept something you say, you are passing the baton and it now becomes a part of him or her. It is almost as if you didn't have to say it, because by accepting it he or she is taking responsibility for it and is running with it. You are in effect putting words in his or her mouth, aren't you? And why does this work well? Because he or she believes what is in his or her mouth—every word of it—but he or she won't necessarily believe everything you say. So, if you want the customer to believe you, get him or her to say it. It's that simple. Quite likely, he or she will tell his or her people about it later, as if he or she had known about it for years, thus impressing them and himself or herself in the bargain.

Third, the repeated yes is the verbal equivalent of getting a foot in the door. If you don't get the customer to open the door in the first place, how can you possibly get into the house later? If the door is only slightly ajar and he or she is peeking at you with reserve and you nevertheless ask the big question, chances are he or she will quickly say, "Let me think it over," and close it.

The more yes's, the more the customer gets into the habit of becoming receptive to your ideas and the wider the door opens. By the time you ask the closing question, he or she will be more likely to step aside to let you into the house, and you have successfully made the sale.

LIMITATIONS OF THE REPEATED YES

As a conventional and persuasive tool, the repeated yes works with everyone, but you need to customize it to your listener. With normal customers you can freely use it in all of its forms. Customers who put a premium on courtesy and good manners by being so themselves respond well to the repeated

yes technique using OK. Use it in a warm and friendly fashion
before asking them to follow your lead. For example, "Try it,
OK?" "Let's look at these carpets here, OK?" "I would like to
have you hold this for a moment, OK?" When it is done
properly, the customer will find you concerned and gracious,
even charming, just as he or she is or would want to be.

HOSTILE CUSTOMERS

Some customers are critical or suspicious for their own
good reasons. They can negatively affect your attitude. That
along with your time are your two greatest sales assets. Therefore, when it comes to these customers, don't walk into their
punches and haymakers. Sidestep them by turning generalizations into questions. "Nothing comes easy, does it?" "You can't
be too careful, can you?" "What we need in this country are
fewer words and more action, would you agree?" "One day at a
time, correct?" "Nice and easy does it, OK?" "Nothing beats
performance, would you agree?" "You've got to earn your spurs,
true?" "Many are called but few are chosen, true?" "Anyone can
claim anything, right?" "Every company's situation is different,
isn't it?" "Professional managers have only three great resources
to play with, isn't that right?"

Or turn observations into questions, "Your receptionist
always sounds cheerful on the phone, doesn't she?" "The view
from here is really special, isn't it?" "You don't often see a watch
like that, do you?" "From what I read and hear, the business
outlook in the area seems to be brighter, doesn't it?" "We've
really been lucky with our ball teams, haven't we?" "Your fall
collection is better than ever, isn't it?"

For best results, make statements that are undeniably true
and turn them into questions. This will guarantee a yes. "We all
do things for our own good reasons, don't we?" "Everybody has
feelings, don't they?" "There is always a certain percentage, isn't
there?" "Nothing worthwhile was ever invented by a negative
thinker, right?" "The idea is father to the act, isn't it?" "There is
no free lunch, is there?" "If you want to get ahead, you have to
earn it, right?" "All the world loves a bargain, don't they?"

"Everyone wants to be important, right?" So much for its effect on the customer. Now, how about the salesperson?

CURING THE PUSHINESS SYNDROME

How can you be assertive—appropriately aggressive, if you will—without coming across as pushy? How can you get your way without giving offense? How can you remove the pushiness label from your personality profile? The prescription for instant cure is the OK repeated yes technique to be taken in large doses during interviews. What if you take just a few pills? See below.

WHEN IT DOESN'T WORK

The only reason for experiencing failure in using the repeated yes is not using it enough to build the communication bridge. It is not realistic to expect a customer to say yes two or three times over the course of a sales introduction and have him or her say yes at the close.

Give the customer and yourself plenty of opportunities to practice. Nearly anything he or she mentions can be restyled in the form of a question to get a yes. "You mentioned you have been here ten years?" "You said that the investment will not present a problem?" "You said people are a concern in your company?" "You said sales development is important to you?" "You referred to some inequities a while ago?"

IN CASE OF A "NO"

A professional boxer or tennis player wants to know what will and won't work with an opponent. In your work, too, it is important to ascertain what will and won't work with a customer. A "no" clears up a misconception you harbored about his or her situation and steers you back to your target. The multitude of yes responses will far outweigh and outplay the few negatives you will normally hear in an interview. Keep on getting yes responses.

COLD CALLING FOR APPOINTMENTS

"It takes 20 years to become a success overnight," according to Eddie Cantor. Likewise, it takes a lot of little agreements to amount to one big agreement according to human nature.

Jan Ostezan demonstrated cold calling for appointments to live audiences. She was so skilled that anyone could pick a number out of the telephone book and she would immediately dial and get an appointment. When she used a speaker phone, her audience could hear every word.

Jan:	"Hello. Is this Mrs. Liggett?"
Mrs. Liggett:	"Yes, it is.
Jan:	"Mrs. Liggett, this is Jan Ostezan of the Tagrn Corporation. How are you?"
Mrs. Liggett:	"Fine."
Jan:	"Say, we're doing a survey on household cleaners for our client. Have you ever used a product called Fantastic or 99?"
Mrs. Liggett:	"I sure have."
Jan:	"You have?"
Mrs. Liggett:	"Yes."
Jan:	"You sound enthusiastic."
Mrs. Liggett:	"Yes, I am, and I think they're great.
Jan:	"That's what everybody says. I bet you're a good housekeeper."
Mrs. Liggett:	"Why, thank you."
Jan:	"Say, would you be receptive to trying a new product that does as good a job as Fantastic or 99, if you could save a lot of money?"
Mrs. Liggett:	"I sure would, if I could try it first."
Jan:	"OK, I can see you're careful, too."
Mrs. Liggett:	"Yes, I am."
Jan:	"Great. Well, I have some good news. I'll have to be in your area this afternoon anyhow. I show your address as 32 Washington Square, is that right?"
Mrs. Liggett:	"Yes, it is."
Jan:	"Are you going to be there around 4:00 P.M.?"
Mrs. Liggett:	"I'm not sure."
Jan:	"When would you be there for sure, and I'll work my schedule around to fit it in and give you a chance to try it?"

Mrs. Liggett: "At 3:00 P.M."
> *Jan:* "Great, Mrs. Liggett, I'll drop by then. See you at 3:00 P.M., and thanks."

Mrs. Liggett: "Thank you."

See how she positioned each one of her questions to get a yes response from Mrs. Liggett?

A professional interviewing organization reports near-perfect results using a similar technique to the above for attracting prospective clients to its offices. With the help of a consultant they designed a series of yes sets, which sounded appropriately warm, caring, and to the point. Soon they became aware that they had fashioned their own little Pied Piper masterpiece. It's pulling the customers in.

The repeated yes is definitely state-of-the-art. It has a long history. Decades ago a few writers recommended that business conversations and interviews start with a couple of questions that could be answered yes. They make no demands on the listener. Later they recommended yes sets for trial closing questions and for summaries preceding the final close. Its use today is, of course, vastly expanded.

Dick Downs is the kind of salesman of whom legends are made. Possessed of eminently good sense, a refreshing sense of humor, and a brass mine to match, he is an inventor of sorts. What did he invent? A new application of the yes set. Picture this. Dick calls on Harry every six weeks or so for a repeat order. Occasionally Harry stalls or objects in response to a final closing question on a new product. Now, here is Dick armed with sense, humor, and brass. (Try reading this out loud.)

Dick: (In mock seriousness.) Harry, what's the matter with you today?
Harry: (Recognizes Dick's act.) Why? Nothing is the matter, Dick.
Dick: Harry, this is your friend Dick talking to you. Remember me?
Harry: Yeah, I remember you, Dick.
Dick: Harry, don't you know that when you shake your head like this (imitating the nonverbal no), you're straining your neck muscles, and medical science has proved conclusively that it causes headaches and unhappiness. You didn't know that, did you, Harry?
Harry: (Grinning at this put-on.) No, Dick, I didn't.

Dick: Did you know when you move your head up and down like this (demonstrates the affirmative) that this stretches your neck and back muscles and definitely relaxes you and is beneficial to your health? Now do what I do, OK? Up and down, up and down—in unison, Harry. (They both grin now.)

Harry: OK, Dick. Send me an order.

12

Triggers
and Hidden Action
Commands

THE TOP TEN WORDS

For years advertising copywriters and TV audience reaction researchers have known the power of certain words—or *triggers*—as they impinge on the minds of the buying public. Andy Rooney of "60 Minutes" did a humorous commentary about the top ten words in the 1980s. These words have great impact on us, since they trigger us into action more than any other, which is of course what buying and selling are all about. No one suggests that there is anything underhanded or manipulative in their use. They're common words, to which we all like to listen. They hold our interest better than others. In the order of preference, they are "new," "natural," "light," "save," "free," "rich," "real," "fresh," "extra," and "discover," as in "Discover our new and natural taste treat, light in flavor, rich in texture, a real bargain that saves time and effort, and includes a coupon in the package for a free gift."

Other trigger words probably are "now," "power," "simple," "unforgettable," "unique," "self-confidence," "be yourself," "enjoy," "number 1," "guarantee," "success" and "easy."

Why just these words? We associate them with interesting and favorable experiences of the past that we would like to have more of. Each of us has a word preference. Topflight salespeople know how to listen for our favorites and use them to plug into experiences to which they relate.

"SPAREGRASS"

As an example, my family appointed me head of the freedom garden I was about to establish in back of the house. I scouted for assistance and soon located a retired handyman of my acquaintance. He and his wife Laura loved asparagus but called it "sparegrass." Everyone in my family remembered sparegrass. Accompanied by our wives, we surveyed the area and found it suitable.

"What kind of vegetables do you and Laura like?" I asked.

"Oh, most any kind. Tomatoes and corn, maybe beans and maybe potatoes, and some watermelon."

"How about sparegrass?" I queried.

"Oh, we like that best of all. 'Course it takes a couple of years to get ready.

"All right. What say if I rent the tiller and buy the seed, and you tilled the garden and looked after it? Then you take whatever you want and what's left we take?"

They hesitated, so I continued the conversation.

"About how much sparegrass seed should I get?"

"Oh, we'll take care of that," they brightened. "They'd charge you too much in the stores."

This is how we got our vegetable garden.

ROSEBUD

To me, perhaps the most memorable illustration of all is in the movie *Citizen Kane,* which incidentally was just named "Picture of All Time" by 25 international film critics. It is supposed to be a fictionalized account of the life of William Randolph Hearst and ended on one word. That word was "Rosebud" which was stencilled on a children's sled and symbolized the moment of greatest happiness in the character's life. The movie ended with a picture of Rosebud.

Whenever an event, a sound, a word, a view, or a smell causes our minds to associate it with a previous event, that previous event is said to be marked. This may explain the déja vu (seen before) experiences most of us have, where a house or a person or whatever so closely resembles one from the past as to trigger in us the illusion that we have encountered it before.

When you pay close attention to your customer, you can notice those particular experiences, good feelings, and words that seem to have a special meaning to him or her, much like the trigger words "new," "natural," and others. To the customer, these experiences and words ring a bell, the bell of familiar, pleasant, and positive experiences. By marking the particular experiences and good feelings in some way, you will anchor them into your customer's mind and as a result improve the effectiveness of your sales effort.

Trigger techniques work by forming an association between two events, so that the mention of one of them (or flashing an image or using a sound) will automatically trigger the memory of the other. Words are perhaps the most common markers in our lives. Think of the words "confidence" and "motivation" (two important words). Actually these words are only sounds, and these sounds are totally meaningless to anyone who has not learned English. However, they have become meaningful to us, because we associate them with pleasant feelings and experiences of value. Think of the last time you were "sold" on attending an inspirational sales rally. Undoubtedly the brochure and the speaker used words like "inspiration," "confidence," and "motivation" to trigger you. You can use powerful markers, too, in your sales work to get your customers to recall certain good feelings.

Triggers offer valuable things for salespeople. First, they enable you to sequence what you want your customer to experience. You may want your customer to have increased interest in your product, then feel that the competitor's products aren't as good as yours, then to have a sense of urgency about buying it now. This is a simple example, but you could mark each step as your customer went through it. And at the close, trigger those markers to get the customer to have all of these experiences in a condensed and fast-paced sequence. Top salespeople do this often, and with the exercises given in this section you will learn how to do it yourself.

A second advantage is the ability to allow you to appear less intense. No one likes a pushy salesperson, and those salespeople who know how to use triggers never have to be pushy. Triggering can be so casual that it completely escapes detection. Think of this situation: A salesman is having a customer describe every feature she likes about her office computer. As the customer mentions specific features the salesperson nods his head in a special way and says in a low, soothing tone, "That's right." Since the customer is talking about things she likes about her computer, the reinforcement "That's right" causes in her feelings of satisfaction. The salesperson continues saying, "That's right."

Now the salesperson presents his new computer. At the close of the sale, as the customer continues to question, the salesperson nods his head in that special way and says, "That's right," in that soothing tone of voice. He triggers the marker as often as he can. Nodding his head and saying "That's right" have become associated with the customer's own feelings of contentedness and satisfaction. When the salesperson nods his head and says, "That's right," he brings back those feelings— back to the close where they are needed.

Here the triggers were visual and auditory. The visual marker was the sight of the salesperson nodding his head. The auditory marker was the sound of the words, "That's right." A feeling trigger could be touching the person's arm or shoulder when she is having a positive experience or pleasant memory. When touched later on the same spot, the good feeling returns.

Trigger techniques are as effective in sales work as they are in real life. Do you have a special song or a special perfume or after-shave lotion? What makes them special? They have become marked. The special song may remind you of your first romance; the special perfume or after-shave lotion will remind you of a special person.

Have you ever recalled an event while doing something completely unrelated? It may have puzzled you, because you were unaware of what triggered this memory. You might have been working at your desk and suddenly caught yourself daydreaming about a vacation. What triggered it? The noise of an airplane high above, of which you weren't even aware? The sound of the jet engines was the trigger that brought back the memory of the trip.

This brings up another important point about triggers: They normally are beyond the detection of the conscious mind.

It was the unconscious mind that detected the sound of the plane and automatically associated it with the vacation. It is the unconscious aspect of triggers that gives them their power.

The fact that the unconscious mind remembers triggers is what allows top producers to be subtle and nonpushy in their sales work. When a customer is having a good feeling or memory, the salesperson marks it, so that he or she can call up that positive feeling or memory in the customer. When the salesperson later triggers that marker, the customer reexperiences that good feeling. Because this is done through the unconscious mind, the customer doesn't know consciously what is happening and welcomes it. All the customer knows is that he or she feels good.

The process of marking events and feelings works with everyone. It is part of being human to make connections and associations between things. However, triggers differ in their impact on customers.

For some the visual markers, such as nodding your head, rolling your pencil in your fingers, rubbing your eyebrows, or any other kind of visual cue, triggers their positive feelings and memory.

For others, avoid visual markers, especially for customers who don't see well. We are not talking about vision itself—they may have 20–20 vision and still not see well. You can tell who they are: people who continually look down, close their eyes, or daydream. They don't seem to notice what is happening around them. If you tried to use visual markers with them, you would not be very effective. For people who don't see very well, use auditory (sound) markers or action–feeling (touch) markers.

There are customers who don't want to be touched, although these are much rarer than most salespeople realize. Most human beings truly enjoy a light touch on the arm or shoulder and associate this with friendship. Professional salespeople might reexamine the advantages of using this powerful form of nonverbal communication. You can readily tell who among your customers doesn't want to be touched. They tend to give you a lot of span by standing far away from others. Often they hold their bodies in a rigid position and look tense. When shaking hands, they stretch their arm out to keep the other person at a distance. These signs tell you not to touch, but to use visual or auditory anchors instead.

Finally, avoid using auditory (sound) markers with people who don't hear well. If they are constantly saying "Huh?" and asking you to repeat yourself, you have a bad listener. Use visual and feeling markers with this type of person.

WHEN IT WORKS—WHEN IT DOESN'T WORK

The best way to use markers is also the simplest. Early in the sales interaction, elicit some good feelings or memories in your customer. Ask him or her to tell you about a favorite hobby or sport. When you can see that look of enjoyment or satisfaction on his or her face, you apply triggers. You can say in a special tone of voice, "That's great." Or you can widen your eyes and nod your head to create a visual marker. You can roll a pencil between your fingers. The number of markers at your disposal is limited only by your imagination. What's important is to apply a trigger and call up the good feelings in the customer. When you later use your trigger again, the customer will reexperience the desirable feelings and memories and will transfer them to your product or service.

In summary, plan to set up one or two positive triggers early in the sales interview and use your push-button again near the close to redial those good feelings.

On occasion you may pick up negative triggers unknowingly, perhaps a facial expression that reminded your customer of the way his or her father looked just before he was ready to explode. Or you may tap your pen on the desk in a way that irritates the customer. Here pen tapping is a negative trigger. Perhaps his or her high school teacher did that when detaining him or her after hours for improper conduct. When you tap your pen his or her unconscious mind recalls earlier feelings. The customer probably won't even understand it himself or herself. All he or she will know is that he or she doesn't like you.

What do you do in this case? First, be aware and learn to detect it. You won't be able to do anything unless you immediately detect when you are losing or irritating the customer. Often average salespeople lack awareness until too late in the game. Undoubtedly the customer has flashed several signals and warnings before then. Work on increasing the size of your radar dish and become aware of what's happening. The moment your customer is losing interest, apply instant replay. Did you offend him or her in some way? Did you knock your competition? Did you just start tapping your pencil? Did you use a certain facial expression? Did you rub your hands together in a certain fashion? Did you use a particular word? Any one of these can be a powerful negative trigger. If you use a word like "unreliable," your customer may automatically think of an unreliable car that gave him or her problems. The customer will feel badly and some of those bad feelings may interfere with his or her appreciation of the product or service you are trying to sell.

Since words are powerful triggers, strive to use positive words. There are many ways of saying something. Select the positive way of saying it. When comparing a competitor's product or service with yours, say it's not as reliable as yours and avoid calling it unreliable. Stress the positive, which is that your product is reliable. Don't focus on the negatives of anyone or anything. Remember, a knock is a boost, and you can tell more about a person by how he or she talks about others, than by what he or she says about himself or herself. If the other product or company is not up to par, your customer will figure this out by the lack of positive statements you make. You don't have to take risks by being negative. Little things like this can make all the difference in the world in determining how much a customer will accept and trust a salesperson.

How can you increase your customer's sensitivity? A simple way is to study what unsuccessful salespeople do. Throughout this book our focus is on studying the most successful salespeople available to learn what they do that others don't. Now we have the one instance when observing average salespeople pays off. They have a special skill. They are adept at triggering negative emotions in customers with inappropriate statements and behavior. Notice their lack of awareness and sensitivity to others. Observe their lack of flexibility. Recognize that they don't adjust to these differences in customers. Notice their limited range. Whom do they remind you of? A boxer who can't adjust to his opponent's style. Could a football team in the NFL even make it to the top if it didn't scout its numerous opponents? No way! Increase your sensitivity to the power of triggers, and increase your ability to use them systematically.

One of the best uses of triggers is to copy the customer's triggers. Notice what he or she does when feeling really well or thinking of something that makes him or her happy. Does the customer rub his or her chin, explode in a quick short laugh, turn up the corners of his or her mouth in a special way, or take a deep breath and sigh? Whatever it is, store it in your memory bank. This is his or her positive trigger. For the customer it already has an unconscious association with feeling well. All your work has been done for you. You can copy this positive trigger and use it yourself. The customer's unconscious mind will form this connection when you rub your chin or smile in that certain way. Customers are constantly giving a wealth of information about who they are and what they value. Use this information. Since it is part of the person, it becomes compelling when it is repeated back to him or her and helps you make the sale.

HIDDEN ACTION COMMANDS

An Aspirin in a Jellybean

For the first time in memory a certain public corporation's request for rate increases had been rejected by the Public Service Commission. In order to maintain high-quality service they needed more cash flow, and they needed it fast. The simplest way was to get more sales. They decided to do so by having their union installers and repair people sell extra equipment to the customers they were already servicing. We were appointed to help develop the sales. It was a cliff-hanger from the start, until selling became fun. Sales successes were frequent, customer hassles were minimal, and the sales conversation was brief and professional.

After field testing a variety of methods we found one that seemed to suit everybody. The installers and repair people would ask the customer offhandedly, "Just suppose you can have extra extensions anywhere in your home or office. Where would you put them?"

This question was the key to the lock. Most customers reacted favorably. Some also needed to hear, "Just suppose you can have any one of these models. Which would you select?" These quickie conversation starters helped solve the cash flow problem as sales grew in multiples.

In their customary fashion our participants had at first rejected this approach out of hand. But as luck would have it, the most diminutive person in the group reported at the next meeting that she never once missed a sale with this approach. That broke down the dam, and they were willing to listen.

To convince everybody, we cast them individually in the role of customer and had them experience the question themselves. Soon many fashioned their own versions and did a good job. Selling became fun, success was frequent, and concern about wasting time or encountering unpleasant reactions was laid to rest. It worked.

What made these questions so productive yet inoffensive? There are several reasons. Customers seemed flattered when asked for their opinions. They enjoyed thinking about improving their homes or offices. The "Just suppose" was nonthreatening. Best of all, the customer practically told the installer how to sell him or her. These are all important reasons. But one was left unanswered. Why did this question grip the listener? What was its attraction?

In our innocent ignorance we had played with verbal dynamite. The installers and repair people were using hidden action commands and nobody realized it. And before you blame us too readily, allow me to suggest that you, too, have probably used hidden action commands without knowing it. All you knew was that you walked away with the contract.

The term *hidden action command* sounds like a contradiction, doesn't it? How can you give a command to anyone without their knowing it loud and clear?

A hidden action command is a strong suggestion that you can place in a sentence in such a way as to escape detection. It's the chocolate-coated vitamin pill. It's the jellybean-covered aspirin you give your dog. It allows you to voice a command indirectly without giving offense. Yet its impact will be close to a direct order. At once elegant and persuasive, it is an instrument of great flexibility. With it the sales virtuoso can create whatever suggestion or command he or she needs anywhere in his or her presentation from opening to close.

How can you apply this to your customers? In the opening you may want to involve your customer more actively in thinking about your program in a positive way.

- "Most successful investors *make a quick decision, Steve.*"
- "Many top supervisors *follow through on a scheduled basis, Mary.*"
- "Only professional managers *read this newsletter, Gary.*"
- "A hacker tends to *recognize the uniqueness of this design, Max.*"

For added impact, many top producers pronounce the hidden action command differently from the rest of the sentence. As they start the command portion, they look directly at the customer and speak firmly and deliberately. The effect is powerful. You would do well to follow their example.

Use hidden action commands at the close, too:

- "Just *visualize the fun she'll have with this toy.*"
- "Can you *think how much business you'll get with this item?*"
- "When you *decide to pay the difference,* you can live in a better area, Mr. and Mrs. Van Arsdale."
- "You'll own it, Jack, when you *put away $100 a month.*"
- "On the basis of these figures, you could *increase your investments, Robert.*"
- "I don't know if you'll *buy this insurance from me.*"

What can you do with suspicious customers? Or with people who don't like to be told anything? Or with those who are reluctant or resistant? Or with procrastinators?

Hidden action commands take care of these problems neatly. You don't have to ask a customer to consider or do anything directly. You can ask indirectly. Top producers excel in indirect communication. They get people to change their minds and leave smiling. Hidden action commands escape detection and therefore resistance. They work because they are fully processed and impinge on the customer's unconscious. Hidden action commands are the verbal equivalents of subliminal visual images, which are flashed on a screen for only fractions of a second. Even though they escape detection by the conscious mind, they are taken in and understood by the unconscious mind, resulting in a powerful impact on a person's feelings and thoughts.

Use Your Good Judgment

Hidden action commands work with all people. Depending on your sales skill, you may not want to use this technique with everyone, however. With interested and cooperative customers, there is little call for hidden action commands. Speaking in a plain and direct manner will do fine. Why use a hammer for a thumbtack?

On rare occasions hostile customers, looking for reasons to vent their feelings, may actually question a hidden action command. For example, a drug detailer says to a physician, "Many doctors *prescribe Tagamet to patients with ulcers.*" The know-it-all doctor may challenge with, "Are you stating that I should prescribe Tagamet?" The detailer can easily handle the question. "That, of course, is up to your professional judgment, Doctor. I am sharing with you what many other doctors are doing now." Since both hostile and aggressive people tend to focus excessively on themselves, the hidden action command is an excellent vehicle for communicating with them. It takes the focus off them. You gain leverage by talking about other people. You make suggestions indirectly, and as a consequence their unconscious minds will be programmed with your idea. In the preceding example, even though the drug detailer said, "I'm sharing what other doctors are doing now," the doctor's unconscious mind nevertheless was fertilized with the idea. Remember, the human mind is in some ways like a tape recorder. Once an idea is recorded there, it stays.

When applying the hidden action commands, the question is not "Will they work?" as much as "how hard do you want them to work?" At times your customers can be moved with a feather. In those instances speak the words in your customary manner.

When you want hidden-action commands to have the effect of a bulldozer, underscore them in order to draw more unconscious attention to them. It matters little how you speak, as long as you pronounce them differently. You can go slower or faster, speak more loudly or in a whisper, or even adopt a slight accent. The purpose is to draw more attention to them. Avoid going overboard, however, or the customer may notice what you're doing and the effect will no longer be subconscious. Practice will make perfect. We've heard top salespeople use hidden action commands in strange and unusual tones of voice without alerting a customer's conscious attention. The total impact is powerful.

Put Them in a Story

A sophisticated form of using hidden action commands is to include them in a sales story or sales metaphor. You can have a story character say something that you could never get away with yourself. For example, you could talk about a neighbor who said, "It's very important to *buy $100,000 of insurance.*"

Customers love hearing stories. They drop all of their defenses and prepare to be entertained.

As with everything else, hidden action commands may not work when they are used unskillfully. Here the salesperson may be too heavyhanded and too direct. Practice using this technique, and you shall indeed be well rewarded in your personal and in your professional life. If in doubt, remember it is preferable to err on the side of being too indirect or too discreet, rather than too direct or obvious. You can always change your tactics later if you have to.

PART IV
TECHNIQUES FROM
SALES SUPERSTARS

13

The Ultimate
Persuasive Tools:
Stories and Metaphors

I was absent the day our high school class took up metaphors. A *metaphor* is a figure of speech, I learned later. When you say "iron horse" instead of "train" or "time flies" instead of "time passes" or "A Mighty Fortress Is Our God" instead of "I'm secure in the Lord," you are painting figures of speech. When football coach John Madden says, "This guy's elevator doesn't go all the way to the top floor," that is easy to understand for anyone whose elevator does. When people ask Jim Sirbasku what he does for a living, he replies, "I'm a lead miner." "A lead miner—here in Texas?" they ask. "Not that kind of a lead miner," he chuckles. "I take the lead out of people's seats." That is Jim's figure of speech for saying he is a motivator of sales people.

Here are some other metaphors:

- "Her hands are tied."
- "She doesn't wear the pants in the family."
- "Remember that comes straight from the horse's mouth."
- "He isn't exactly being paid a gastronomical sum to eat his words."
- "So pull the plug on him."
- "He doesn't have a snowball's chance in hell."
- "He couldn't sell his way out of a paper bag."
- "That will be curtains for him."

Not all metaphors are alike. New metaphors are like new clothes, and people are apt to notice and smile, while the old ones are a little threadbare and won't quite do the job for you.

Some of the most memorable sales stories and metaphors are the creation of inspirational speakers and authors. One great motivator said, "Logic shrinks in the mind of the listener, quickly to be forgotten, while emotion expands like the Incredible Hulk and seizes the imagination."

"Prove it," you say.

How about this?

When hundreds of people are perishing in battle, that's front-page news. Nobody really knows them as individual personalities, only as a group of victims. But let one little boy fall into an abandoned mine shaft where rescue is doubtful, and you have all the ingredients of headlines. Before he's rescued you'll know the child's name, parents, friends, dogs, and favorite toys. This is human interest. This is an emotional event that deeply touches us all. That's a story. Here is one in a lighter vein.

Chris was in the market for a word processing unit. "How do you use this thing?" she asked the computer salesman.

He said, "Just boot the disk here into the RAM, and the CPU does the rest."

"You're kidding," she said. "Doesn't anybody speak English any more?"

"You're right. I was only kidding," he replied. "I was quoting from one of our brochures. You see this disk? It's like a record on your turntable. You want to hear Beethoven's Fifth, you've got to pick the right record. You want to listen to Elvis, you've got to have a different record. Instead of calling it a record, call it instructions. You want word processing, or a financial package, you need the right instructions for the computer. Get it?"

Now he was beginning to reach her. She had bought stereo sets before and could relate to what he was saying. He was using an analogy. Many top producers tend to express themselves in analogies, metaphors, and sales stories, because they bring the humdrum and commonplace, the technical and complex within easy reach of the customer's comprehension.

Great salespeople know how to put a face on Mr. Everyman. They'll put shoe leather on his feet, emotion in his belly, laughter on his lips, a twinkle in his eyes, and quotables in his mouth. Mr. Everyman has now been transformed into a personality that's alive. He reminds us of someone we know and relate to. For example, in inspiring an audience, one speaker proceeded as follows.

"In a way," he said, "all of us are wheels. Some of us are small tricycle wheels, some of us are car wheels, and a few of us are huge earth-mover wheels. Now you'll notice that a little wheel has to turn a lot more often to cover the same distance than a big wheel. That's why most of us want to be big wheels. Less wheel spinning, you see. How does a little wheel become a big wheel? Visualize a wheel with seven spokes. What happens when you make each spoke longer and stronger? The wheel becomes larger. Now one of the spokes is for mental growth, the other for career development, the third for health and physical well-being, the fourth for warm and close family life, the fifth for spiritual growth and moral conduct, the sixth for recreation and having fun, and the seventh spoke is for financial independence and peace of mind in retirement. Take care that you keep your spokes in balance, so that your wheel stays well rounded. You wouldn't want to hobble down a road on bouncy wheels, now, would you?" That's a metaphor.

Our country is currently embarked on a crusade for quality. And still a lot of people are touchy about the subject, especially those who don't have to compete with the Japanese or Germans. The question is, "How can you sell someone on quality as long as the bank or the hospital they are managing is getting by?" Phil Crosby, the inventor of the Zero Defects Program and author of *Quality Is Free* and *How to Get Your Own Sweet Way*, has succeeded in taking a mundane subject and attracting immediate attention with statements, here abbreviated: Quality has much in common with sex. Everyone is for it. Everyone feels they understand it. Everyone thinks execution is only a matter of following natural inclinations. And everyone feels that all problems are caused by other people."

Phil is preaching a gospel here, but the way he puts it—by likening it to sex—makes it not only entertaining but quotable.

He is using a figure of speech. Typical of all great persuaders, he first gets your attention and then gets you to fully understand the impact of the Zero Defects concept. After he gets your attention, he wants to sell you on the notion that even 1 percent variable in quality is unacceptable. Here is how he does it, paraphrased: "To clone people, take DNA out of their cells to reproduce them. The difference between the DNA formula to make a gorilla and a human being is only 1 percent. If your genetic engineering has a quality level close to 1 percent, you'll never know whether you get a gorilla or Raquel Welch."

Here Phil did it again with metaphor and story. It was Crosby's ex-boss and early convert at ITT, Harold Geneen, who was quoted as saying, "Quality is free. And it's not only free, it's the most profitable product line we have." What a great metaphor!

Here is another. An insurance salesman was defusing an objection by a young client, who had seemed to prefer buying from a smaller, more personalized company. "It's like taking you and your family on a long voyage across the Atlantic Ocean, and you want to get from here to England, and you have a choice of either going on this tug boat here or on the *Queen Mary*. Which one would you feel safest on?" The prospect decided on the *Queen* and bought.

Sales stories and metaphors work in four ways. First, they grip the customer's attention because they're like a movie. You're telling a story. You are not talking dry facts.

Second, they work by simplifying things for the customer. Even highly intelligent people like things to be kept simple. A sales story makes the point neatly.

Third, they get the customer's emotions going. As you know, most people buy primarily for emotional reasons, not logical ones. A good sales story can trigger the emotions of pride of ownership, safety, love, adventure, or anything else that's positive.

Finally, they are memorable. A good story will stay in the customer's mind long after everything else is forgotten.

Metaphors, stories, analogies, and anecdotes have been used all over the world for thousands of years to influence people. Socrates and Homer taught with stories. Jesus spoke in parables. Abe Lincoln and Ronald Reagan have made their most powerful points through metaphors and anecdotes. The Harvard Business School uses case histories.

For salespeople, effectiveness depends on quickly developing good feelings in the customer. Good feelings can influence a customer without his or her conscious awareness. They make their points by creating a comfortable atmosphere and rarely cause resistance. And practically no one objects to a well-chosen story.

You can have a character in a story make a point that you cannot make directly as a salesperson. You can tell a prospect about someone who is enthusiastic about your service.

Gene Verity's experience serves as an example. Soon after installing his management engineering system in an operation, he would have his client, the CEO, make appointments for him with new prospects in the industry. Did he have much trouble closing the new prospect? No. Whenever he did encounter some reluctance, he'd simply talk about how tickled his referror was with the new material or energy savings, or the reduction in tardiness and absenteeism. That would prove reassuring enough to overcome any hesitation on the part of the prospect and result in a new assignment.

WHY IT WORKS

We have long been aware about the impact and use of stories and metaphors. Yet, until recently, little was known about how they work and how to construct them. The works of popular sales trainers like Tom Hopkins and Zig Ziglar make extensive use of stories, metaphors, and examples. That is the most powerful thing they do. Audiences tend to remember their stories, as much as or more than their techniques.

Stories and metaphors click in the minds of the listeners because of the relevance of the relationship between the characters. You can make the same point with a tale about elves and princesses as between businesspeople or among family members.

Charlie Salzman sold industrial detergents to large bakeries in Pennsylvania 30 years ago. The purchasing agent was a grandmotherly type, to whom he told the following true story:

"Mrs. Wiedemeyer, my company is holding a sales contest and the first prize is a TV set. I showed the announcement to my little daughter, Maureen, and she was all excited. She said, 'Are you going to win that TV set, Daddy?' So I said, 'Do you want me to win a TV set for you, Maureen?' And you should have seen her. She was hopping up and down. She was throwing her arms around me. And I told her, 'Yeah, I guess your Daddy is going to win a TV set for you.' Now, I don't know if I'll win it or not, but little Maureen is going to get her TV set, you can bet on that."

Mrs. Wiedemeyer was enchanted and visibly moved. She said, "You know, we have a little granddaughter, and we're just crazy over her. Tell you what. Send us ten drums of your Kra-Z-Kleen just before your contest ends. That way you might win that TV set for little Maureen."

People think in terms of mind pictures. That's why metaphors and stories are so powerful. They play directly into how the human mind works, since it customizes whatever it encounters. When you hear the word *dog*, you recall a particular dog—a mutt, a collie, a German Shepherd, or a poodle. What kind would you think of?

In the same way, you customize a story or a metaphor by automatically relating it to your life and experience. It takes no effort; your mind does it for you. When you hear a story about someone's sales award, you'll remember yours. You identify with it. The only way you can understand the experience of any other human being is by relating it to a real or hoped for experience of your own. Sales metaphors work so well because they help you to visualize and relive the experience.

When your prospect hears a story about a happy customer, he or she will recall the time he or she was well pleased with a product. This memory carries with it a positve feeling, and because it's emotional it expands in his or her consciousness. Stories and metaphors work by systematically bringing up good feelings in customers. By telling the right stories you can get your customers to resonate to the emotional appeal of their choice. This leads them from feelings of security to conviviality, to status, to happiness, to pride of ownership, or whatever. It's the fun route to motivational selling, a route that top producers use to influence customers. Some consistently effective sales-people make their sales largely through stories, volunteering relatively little product knowledge yet making lots of sales. To salespeople unfamiliar with the power of metaphors and sto-ries, this is a revelation.

They feel that customers buy on the basis of return on investment, price, or competitive bids—in other words, on logic. But often it isn't so. Now more than ever, customers shop for value, of which price is only a part of the total picture. That's why some companies become wealthy and their competitors don't.

Come to think of it, aren't storytellers and metaphor magicians just a little wiser, a little more realistic in the ways of humanity? They know that people do not buy on logic or do logical things. People are emotional, and stories bring up feelings that lead to a successful sale. It is as simple as that. Human beings love stories and metaphors. Your customers will love you for telling them stories and will buy from you. When you and others compete for the same business, everything else being equal, you'll make the difference—with the right stories.

Of course, some stories work better than others, and so the question is, which works best with whom? This is probably the most profitable and enjoyable exercise you can experiment with. Here are some hints.

In constructing stories of your own, be sure they are relevant to the listener so that they can easily identify with them. Tailor the language and the word pictures to appeal to their communication channel—visual, auditory, or action–feel-ing. Keep the stories simple, even if your listeners are well educated. When telling a joke, make sure that your story has a message and makes a point.

People love good stories, and they call them by all kinds of names: nursery rhymes, legends, myths, fables, fairy tales, novels, film scripts, science fiction, modern romances, plays, soap operas, musicals, and music lyrics. Billy Joel, popular singer and composer, was made an honorary Allentown, Pennsylvania, citizen and given the key to the city for a 60-word song, which is a masterpiece of pacing. As the saying goes, it tells it like it is," and 644 fans gave him a standing ovation for what he sang and how he sang it.

When your customer needs the approval of a committee of three before he or she can make a decision, tell a story about a group of three statesmen or three entrepreneurs who launched a successful project together. Or, if your customer works on a limited budget, tell about a family or a young businessman who in spite of meager funds made a good choice. President Ronald Reagan told stories about how, as governor of California, he handled budget problems. The message was that he intended to do the same in Washington. The implication was that a previous budget problem in his home state was analogous to the nation's current budget problem.

Even the best sales metaphor or story can miss the target unless it is properly sequenced. A story may be great in grabbing the customer's attention, yet fail to grip him or her in the close. A story may be just the ticket for defusing an objection but not qualify as support of a product or feature.

Each customer goes through a certain series of feelings before he or she arrives at a decision to buy. It is like dialing a phone number. You may know all of the right digits, but as long as you don't touch them in their proper sequence, you won't reach the right number.

The same is true in sales. Did you know that some customers need to feel somewhat frustrated before they can make a purchase? That's true. And others need to feel curious, understood, or a variety of other things. You can tell a story to bring up any feeling you want in the customer. You can even bring up sadness or anger by telling a story if you wish.

The key is to tell stories in their proper sequence. Your customer may need to feel curiosity, a sign of interest; then frustration, a sign of tension to have a need satisfied; then satisfaction, a sign you have offered a satisfactory solution—before he or she buys. You can tell three different stories to access each of these feelings in their proper order. This is what top producers strive to do. To the untrained eye, it looks as easy as a golf pro birdie-ing a hole. Nothing to it. All you do is tell stories, make customers laugh and feel well, and presto—another sale. But there is a lot more preparation in it than meets the eye. Top salespeople are interior decorators of the commonplace. Their product or service may be ordinary, but against the background of colorful language and skillful stories they make it look positively irresistible. Remember, stories can be told in a variety of ways. Even those from the Bible have been simplified to a point where a five-year-old understands them. So tailor them to fit your customer.

Finally, make sure the content of your story is appropriate. Telling a sexist story to woman or a racist story to a minority group member shows poor taste and poor judgment. It will not help your sales. And equally insensitive is to tell stories about corporate policy to a farmer or about seed or fertilizer to a CEO, unless his or her company happens to be in that business. So keep your story content on your customer's turf. Remember, some subjects are of interest to almost everyone, especially those dealing with good food, money, security, health, self-esteem, and feeling well. Topics such as sports, animals, basic human interactions, family life, gardening, or traveling are also general enough to appeal to almost every listener.

Ben Feldman of New York Life is a case in point. He was the first life insurance salesman to break the $1 million annual income barrier. He became wealthy in part because he rediscovered and innovatively applied a topic of unusual interest—money. As he tells it, he approaches his client with, "I want to talk to you about money," and so saying opens a luxuriously bound three-ring notebook. On the inside front cover is a window with a real $1000 bill behind it. Instant interest. Perfect pacing. "Is this real? Can I touch it?" the prospect would ask. Ben would pull it out and hand it to him or her. Again, he'd lead the conversation back to money, which he had made so real. He would mention its importance to people he knew in circumstances similar to the prospect's. He was being relevant, because the prospect could put himself or herself into the picture Ben had provided.

See yourself as a collector of these verbal gems. Here are some hints. In constructing stories of your own, make certain that they are relevant to the listener, so that he or she finds it easy to identify with the story and the people in it. Tailor the language and the word pictures to appeal to his or her communication channel—visual, auditory, or action–feeling. Keep your stories simple, even if the prospect is well educated. Finally, recall or create stories and metaphors for specific purposes, such as developing interest, for stalls and objections, and whatever situation you may find. Check them for their emotional impact, so that you can generate the kind of emotion you want for your customer. Get some for every sales occasion. You'll be wealthy in more ways than one.

14

Humor,
Surprise, and Confusion:
Fun While Selling

STARTLING STATEMENTS

Humor, surprise, and confusion have one common de-
nominator: They're startling to the customer and often do a
better job as tension breakers and mind-set breakers than
scotch and water. They move things off dead center. Let's look at
some just for fun.

A man visits a Phone Center Store in Wichita and spies a
section in the showroom called Phun Center. Smiling, he
approaches the sales desk and says, "How can I get even with
my landlord? I live in an apartment, and he wouldn't let me
keep my dog." Perhaps he thought he would stump the sales
clerk. Instead, she said, "I've got just the phone for you." And
she sold him a Snoopy phone. Now he is agitating his landlord
by telling him he's got a dog again.

George Steinberger, record-breaking life insurance salesman and author of *If You Don't Mind My Asking*, describes 33
ways to defuse objections. When a prospect says, "I can do
better with my money in real estate," he asks, "Oh, how much
real estate were you planning on buying today for $5 a week?"
That's both humorous and startling, and it gets the interview
back on track.

Paul J. Meyer, master motivator, sales record breaker, and
founder of Success Motivation, Inc., shared this story with me
one day. An acquaintance of his was a Bible salesman in the

South. He was a good salesman, but there was one objection he couldn't handle and that was "Brother Jones, the wife and I aren't going to make a decision tonight. We'll first have to pray on it and see what the Lord says. You call me tomorrow." Here is what Paul's friend came up with: "There is no need to do that, Brother Hillyard. I've already talked to the Lord, and he said it's all right." That so surprised the prospect that he immediately placed an order. Whoever said that selling is not an emotional game?

As a young man one stock broker made house calls, selling mutual funds. His interviews rarely took more than 15 minutes, because he confused his customers by coming straight to the point: "Here you see a chart showing the performance of the ABC Fund over the last ten years. Impressive, isn't it?" The people agreed. "What I've learned is that no matter how detailed a presentation I make, most people say, 'Let me think about it.' So why don't you and I discuss what you want to think about, all right?" The customer would agree. "Is it the size of the company? Is it the management of the fund? Is it me? Or is it only how much you want to invest today?" It was all so different, so unexpected, that they were startled into reacting positively. It was a lean way to sell—few words.

This story appeared in a real estate magazine years ago. A broker talked to the chief executive of a corporation and asked him for a final decision. The chief executive said, "I cannot give you a decision today." The broker replied with a smile, "Mr. Zimmerman, I could believe that if you weren't the man who sits behind this executive desk. You're used to making bigger decisions than that all the time." Startled, the chief executive nevertheless felt complimented and readily capitulated with "OK, let's do it." The broker called this the complimentary contradiction.

Some years ago a young sales engineer was marketing vapor generators for cleaning the inside of resin-coated tank trucks. The vice-president of operations confronted him, saying, "None of your units is large enough. They should have four times their current capacity."

"How many would you want, if the price is reasonable?" the young engineer asked.

"About two, maybe three, and the price would have to be $2500 each."

The young engineer said, "At that price, I need at least five units to go to my engineering department with."

"But I can only buy three."

The salesman said, "Why don't you call the XYZ Tank Lines to take two. They're friends of yours. You've nothing to lose."

The vice-president was startled and laughed. He placed the call. A few minutes later he informed an equally surprised sales engineer, "You just sold five units."

A hospital equipment salesman had but one item: an ultrasonic unit that was a latecomer on the market. He managed to have the administrator introduce him personally to the head nurse of the department and then began his demonstration. Soon the head nurse would ask, "How many of these units have you sold?"

"Personally, I haven't sold any."

"What? Are you saying we might be the first?"

"Oh no! You see I've learned that you ladies are much better at selling what you want to the administration than I am. Now, if you like to know how it works, I'll help you sell it. I'll be your assistant. So I guess it's going to be up to you."

This surprising switch worked very well, certainly better than if he had tried to shoulder the sales burden alone.

A university hospital regularly bought disposables from George Haber. As he grew in experience, he tried selling big-ticket items but was told to be satisfied with what business he had. One day George surprised the hospital staff by showing up with a surgical table on casters. He set it up and had the head nurse wheel it around. She loved its design and maneuverability. "George," she said, "will it fit through our doors?"

"How many would you want if it did?" asked George, surprising the head nurse and himself with his own question.

"Four," she said.

"You just bought four," said George as he wheeled the unit through the door. "That was the day," he explained later, "when I became a salesman."

Humor, surprise, and confusion are methods of changing the mood of the sales environment. There are times when no amount of product information will get the customer into a buying frame of mind. This is where humor, surprise, and confusion come in.

They work by changing the customer's emotions and perspectives. Humor works by developing good feelings, positive emotions, and a lighter atmosphere. Surprise and confusion work by signaling the customer that he or she does not grasp the situation yet. The customer feels he or she needs more information in order to reestablish his or her equilibrium. Humor, by creating positive emotions, draws the customer closer to the salesperson. It helps develop rapport and trust and opens up a more favorable mutual attitude. It may make him or her more carefree, less tense, more relaxed, and more congenial. Whichever it is, a new and slightly startling experience shuttles him or her away from a fearful and tense mental track. Humor itself involves surprise or mild confusion.

Surprise and confusion show the customer that he or she is not in control as much as he or she thought. Exceptionally rigid people have had a lot of practice ignoring new information that is presented in a straightforward way. How to break this mindset is the problem. Surprise and confusion do that job. Once the customer is in a state of uncertainty, he or she becomes highly receptive. You have now created a climate where you can profitably supply the customer with what he or she needs to know in order to buy.

Humor, surprise, and confusion are a form of mild shock treatment, of course. Watch your voltage, because, effective as they are, they must be used in good taste in terms of your customer's values and beliefs.

We all know from practical experience and psychological studies that human beings buy more for emotional than for logical reasons. This is true even for the highly educated stratum of our population. Once their emotional juices flow in the right direction, they will more readily make a purchase decision. In fact, most of us buy emotionally and afterward become logical for doing it. This is called rationalizing. Humor, surprise, and confusion are a means for reaching and influencing the emotions of human beings.

Why does humor work in sales? People like it. Think of how much money we pay for humor. Some of the most highly paid people in the world are those who can make us laugh. Bob Hope, Johnny Carson, Bob Newhart, and others have become millionaires as a result of their ability to entertain us. Humor helps us forget the drabness of our daily lives. It gives us fresh perspectives. Good humor brings sunshine into our lives. It's an automatic pacing system—we both laugh and share our humanity with one another. Most public newspapers could not survive without comic strips. People who can produce and use humor are rewarded. This is as true in sales as in any other aspect of life. Customers welcome a little laughter and humor, because chances are they already get a lot of practice in keeping the lid on their emotions throughout the day. They are accustomed to handling tension, pressure, and difficult situations. However, laughter will break them wide open. They aren't used to handling laughter and have few, if any, defenses against it.

Another reason for using humor, surprise, and confusion is that they capture the customer's attention. During the early part of a sales interview, one plant manager became absorbed in her own thoughts. After waiting a while, the salesman asked, "Tell me, Linda, why is it that plant managers are so easy to talk to?" The plant manager grinned, paid attention, and bought. She was startled and appreciated the salesman's deftness.

Customers like good surprises. Audiences like mystery guests. Promoters feature special attractions. That's exciting. That gets people to pay attention and march through the turnstiles. How many times have you heard of someone who built a better mousetrap and no one beat a path to their door? To get people to buy, you've got to get them to listen. And to get them to listen, you've got to get their attention. The biggest promoters of the past and present—Bill Barnum, Mike Todd, Bill Veek, and Don Canham—didn't have a better product, nor were they waiting for Santa Claus. But they knew how to attract attention. Here is a recent news event in the sports world.

The University of Michigan stadium holds as many as 106,000 spectators. The football team was away, but Don Canham, the athletic director, wanted to stage a fun afternoon for the fans. So he booked Slippery Rock College from Pennsylvania to play its game in the stadium. Up to that time most Michiganians had probably heard the name Slippery Rock but thought it was a joke. They were surprised. It's not only a good school, but it also played good football. How many spectators came just out of curiosity? 65,000!

Remember Mohammed Ali's "dance like a butterfly, sting like a bee"? Remember his poetry? At one time his was the most recognized face in the world and the biggest drawing card in boxing. Remember the antics of Mark "the Bird" Fidrich, who drew SRO crowds even in the minor leagues? Both athletes are attention getters.

Think of the last time a customer stopped you dead in your tracks when you were selling. What can you do the next time? Try humor to ease tension, surprise to shift the focus, or confusion to make him want to know more. Humor, surprise, and confusion may not get you directly to your goal, but one thing is certain: You'll no longer be dead in the water. You will have something new to work with. Successful salespeople are flexible and take advantage of this element of surprise. It gets attention.

Because surprise and confusion create a need for new input, they are tailor-made for those who wouldn't listen to you otherwise. When competing salespeople use the same language and the same ideas, customers get the feeling that somehow they've sat through this movie before. When you use surprise or confusion, you become distinctive and are remembered.

A truly successful life insurance salesman on the West Coast opens some sales calls with, "Life insurance is a terrible investment." The customer is taken aback. That's not what he or she expected. First, it is opening with a sensational headline. The salesman gets immediate attention. Second, the customer wonders why a sane salesperson would make a statement like that. Third, it seems to reassure him or her that it's not going to be a high-pressure encounter. Fourth, now more relaxed, the customer is more receptive to what the salesman has to say. Fifth, by the end of the interview, the customer feels he or she is

making a good choice by following the salesman's recommendations, puts his or her name on the application, and writes a
check.

NEGATIVE SELLING TECHNIQUES

In the past, sales training specialists have cautioned against
teaching negative selling. In the hands of some neophytes or
salespeople suffering from low self-esteem, it can misfire. You
need a certain kind of cool, like that of a bullfighter who
plunges the blade between the shoulders of the animal.

My neighbor Les Johnson was pursuing a successful career
in financial planning. His income over the previous five years
had quadrupled, and it showed in the way he walked and
carried himself. I described an approach for developing
achievement thinking and behavior to him, but he gave it scant
attention. I wasn't getting through to him. What to do? Negative selling to the rescue. "Of course, Les, you don't need a
program like that. You already are very successful."

He straightened up. "What do you mean, I don't need it?
Maybe I want to be a whole lot more successful than you know.
Now, tell me about it again. I might just want to buy it." And he
did.

You're probably familiar with this version of negative
selling. Let's say a swimming pool contractor was referred to
you by your neighbor. After a site survey, he talks to you as
follows: "Now, Chester, so far as the area is concerned there is
no problem. What it comes down to is style and price of pool.
Now, the people across the street chose the luxury model, but
they let me know that is probably a little bit out of your range.
They thought the economy model might be of interest. It goes
for $8200. Now, we also have the regular model for $10,500."

All the while, you take this in quietly and say, "How much
did you say the luxury model was?"

"Oh, that. That's $12,800."

"OK, build us one." (Message to the neighbor: "I'll show
you who can't afford it!")

Another technique based on surprise and confusion is
negative selling, or reverse selling. It's an instant attention
getter. Here are three examples:

"Why would you want to be any more successful? You're already at the top," surprised and disturbed Les Johnson.

"No sense presenting the luxury pool. You couldn't afford it anyhow," disquieted the swimming pool prospect.

"Maybe you don't want a house and a neighborhood like that. They're pretty fancy," is just a little dismaying to hear. Is the salesperson implying I don't measure up?

In the minds of most customers and salespeople, each has a specific role to play in the sales game. The salesperson is the advocate; the customer is the judge and jury. The salesperson is assertive, even aggressive; the customer is noncommittal and judgmental. The salesperson does the courting; the customer is to be courted. Negative selling means switching roles. The salesperson challenges the customer: "Given your situation, why would you want what I have to offer?" The customer replies, "I'll tell you why." Isn't that surprising? Isn't it great? When the customer gives you his or her reasons why he or she should have your product, that is a lot more powerful than when you come up with your own reasons.

SURPRISE

Often candor and straightforwardness can be surprising to the customer, particularly when the salesperson takes some risk by making himself or herself vulnerable. Here are some illustrations.

Dave Sandler teaches a method that sounds risky but isn't. Here is a paraphrase: "Based on what we discussed, it looks like you have some interest in what we're talking about. Let me ask you a question. On a scale of 0–10, 0 signaling no interest and 10 meaning you're ready to use it, where are you now?" This is a new experience for the customer, who is rating the sales presentation, thus providing valuable feedback to the salesperson.

Here's another approach: "As we discuss this service, I'd like you to do me a favor. I invite your feedback. I want it because I can do a better job for you and save us time. So let me ask you, if you were me, how would you sell this product to you?" The customer is surprised and usually likes the involvement.

Gerhard Gschwandtner, publisher of *Personal Selling Magazine,* tells of the German salesman who begins an interview with a new prospect by saying, "Well, are you ready to buy yet?" You can imagine how this takes customers by surprise. They wonder what this crazy salesman might say next, and they listen carefully to his every word. Moreover, the way he says it is very important. He delivers it with a smile and a little bit of mischief. How can you help but like a man like this? Indirectly, he is saying, "I am self-confident. I am proud of my product. I am not afraid to ask for the order."

In this section, the text and the examples have shown why humor, surprise, and confusion work in helping you to be more flexible and successful. Of all the techniques presented in this book, humor, surprise, and confusion are the ones that must be used with great care. Like all powerful tools, they can be useful or risky, depending on the skill level of the user.

When dealing with joyless, humorless, or grim customers, be careful with your use of humor, surprise, and confusion. Use them only as a last resort. This may be just the thing to brighten the mood. It may be just the thing to create a need for new information or to break out of a circle. It may give the customer a new perspective. The customer may be able to see you in a new light. Don't let the overly serious or grim customer leave your showroom or walk out of your office without first trying humor, surprise, or confusion. Many customers can handle tons of pressure, but if you get them to laugh, it breaks them wide open.

In a similar vein, sell by pacing highly logical customers with logic, reasoning, and product information. Sell them with what they do and the way they think. That failing, you can then turn to humor, surprise, and confusion and a new perspective in your relationship.

If a customer has just suffered a setback or tragedy, pace his or her mood and be sensitive in your humor, surprise, and confusion. These people are already confused, and there is no need to add to it. Often these people are remarkably open to new input, especially when you offer solutions to their problems.

Humor can be especially delicate. When first meeting people, it's wise to avoid it. Later, use it with restraint and know whom you are talking to. Comedians are not always taken seriously. Tastes in jokes vary. A third reason is that jokes frequently put somebody down. Last, joke telling may trap you into entertaining instead of selling. When you do use humor, make certain that the customer will appreciate it and that it serves a purpose.

A well-known speaker addressed his company's annual convention. Using a series of jokes between points, he gradually escalated the risqué factor as well as the decibels on the laugh meter. At the finish he unleashed his blockbuster. The male audience was in an uproar, loving every minute of it. But the management was not pleased. The blockbuster laid an egg so far as future engagements for the speaker were concerned.

Humor, surprise, and confusion work best when they are well timed, presented in a sincere manner, and customized to meet the needs of each particular prospect. Never do anything questionable. While it raises eyebrows it may also backfire. Here are two examples.

A few years ago, I was studying top life insurance producers and the effects of prestige automobiles and custom-tailored clothing as their image projectors of success. I had made an appointment with the most successful life insurance salesman in the area to visit me at 10:00 A.M. I knew about what to expect, or so I thought. A minute or two before 10:00, I heard a car race into my driveway and slam its brakes. A man jumped out of a $20,000 sports car and soon pounded on the door. I was stunned. I let him in, and he introduced himself. He had on a handmade, $1000 raw silk suit, fashioned in an elegant yet conservative style, and he wore a $4000 Rolex watch.

Having studied top sales producers for some years, I must admit he did not fit the mold. I found myself somewhat confused. I needed information to make sense of the new encounter. "How could he possibly be so successful? What is his secret? He must be the best insurance man around. He must really know his stuff. I had better buy my insurance from him."

Without saying a word, the man had my rapt attention. He controlled the situation. Of course, this might not work with everyone. The salesman never once made reference to his car, clothes, or watch. And, surely, some people are not impressed by these trappings. Still, those who are aware of fine clothes and other power symbols could not help but be overcome by the total picture. It was effective.

The other real-life example concerns Dummy Mahan, a fighter who was deaf. In the 1920s, he was a contender for the world welterweight title, going against champion Mushy Callahan. The people selling tickets were having a difficult time attracting attention to the fight. They needed to do something to sell more tickets.

They had it on good medical authority that parachuting a long distance would restore Dummy Mahan's hearing. Apparently, in past cases, great volumes of air rushing through a deaf person's ears had restored hearing. Therefore, to attract more attention to the fight, the people selling tickets decided to drop Dummy Mahan out of an airplane and take pictures of this surprising cure of deafness.

It could have been a nice attention-getting surprise technique if only the parachute had opened. Dummy Mahan started out deaf and ended up dead.

The moral of this true story is that although surprise and confusion are very valuable attention-getting techniques, you should never do anything dangerous. It may be OK to race up to a prospect's business in a very expensive or unusual car, but there is no need ever to do anything that would risk the health or well-being of yourself or anyone else.

Do not be overwhelmed by the complexities of using humor, surprise, and confusion. Don't tell yourself that it isn't worth the effort to learn how to use them. You will find that there are a variety of simple and effective ways of incorporating humor, surprise, and confusion into your repertoire of sales skills. Since they directly affect human emotion, these are some of the most powerful influence techniques available. While you may not use them in every sales call you make, when you need them there is nothing else that can take their place. And if you do not develop some skills in using humor, surprise, and confusion, you risk getting stuck in ruts and greatly limiting your success as a professional salesperson.

15

Defusing
the Toughest
Objections

CHARLIE SUCCEEDS AGAINST THE ODDS

The ad in the *Philadelphia Inquirer* reads, "Technical Sales Representative for AAA-1 Company. Minimum 3–4 years field sales experience. College graduate with degree in chemistry or chemical engineering. Please reply to…"

Sitting in his office, the divisional vice-president, having interviewed several likely candidates, is now facing Charlie, a relaxed, pleasant-looking man of 32.

After some tension-breaking conversation, the vice-president observes, "You don't mention where you went to college in the résumé, Charlie."

"I can't, sir," says Charlie. "You see, I did not go to college."

"I don't get it," says the vice-president. "Doesn't our ad specify a college graduate with a degree in chemistry or chemical engineering?"

"It does, sir," says Charlie evenly, "and I can see where a degree in chemistry may help some people in selling your products. You are probably asking why I am applying for this job even though I don't at first seem qualified. Right?"

"That's right, Charlie. That's what I'm asking."

"I am with a large candy manufacturer. My job is to sell chocolate-covered cherries to offices and retailers. Over the last three years I have been the leading salesman in the Atlantic region. Some of the customers who know me best tell me I have something that isn't taught in college."

"What's that?"

"Common sense and patience, sir. Many college kids nowadays are too impatient. They are in a hurry to get somewhere. I've got patience. That's why I get new accounts and keep my old ones."

The vice-president nods in agreement. He likes what he's hearing. He likes what he sees. Still, he is resolved to stick with the requirements in the ad and soon sees Charlie to the door.

Reaching the lobby, Charlie calmly proceeds to the nearest public telephone and dials the vice-president's office.

"This is Charlie," he announced. "I'm downstairs. I wanted to thank you for the interview and let you know that I'm the guy who has the patience, who loves people, and who loves selling. How about giving patience and common sense a try?"

Somehow, Charlie is making an impact on the vice-president now. "By gosh, Charlie," he hears himself saying. "I believe you. You sold me. Get on the next elevator and see me right away before I change my mind."

This is the beginning of a great career for Charlie. After his first year he consistently outdistances all other sales associates by wide margins, sometimes doubling the next best producer's volume. What is there about Charlie that convinces the vice-president to forego the stated job requirements? Charlie literally gives him a sample of his selling skills. He does not brag; he proves it:

- Displaying calm courage in competing for a job for which he is unqualified (will to win).

- Demonstrating his innovative skills in focusing away from the importance of a chemical background to the importance of past performance, patience, and love for people.

- Putting his self-confidence on the line by calling the vice-president back minutes after a rejection (perseverance).

- Giving a demonstration of his people skills by handling a potentially awkward situation with deftness and style. He maintains a gentle attitude. He guides the vice-president's thinking into areas that were not considered before. He never challenges the job requirements or asks embarrassing questions. He never argues or overwhelms with words.

In other words, Charlie gives a superb performance in the use of mental judo.

WHAT IS MENTAL JUDO?

Mental judo is a technique of disarming or redirecting the opponent's force without seeming to offer resistance. It is analogous to judo, the gentle martial art of self-defense, which allows you to defend yourself without inflicting harm on your opponent. It is a quick way of dealing with stalls and objections. As in judo, the smaller opponent—here the sales representative—helps the larger opponent—here the buyer—land on the mat by force of his or her own weight.

When faced by an opposing force, whether physical or mental, you have three choices: fight, flight, or mental judo. Fight is "when you push me, I will push you back." Flight is "when you push me, I will run from you." Mental judo is "when you push me, I will use your energy to guide you to better solutions."

Suppose your prospect says, "We have dealt with your competitor for several years, and they've seen us through difficult times. We believe in loyalty. That's why we will continue to work with them."

Using mental judo techniques, you answer, "I couldn't agree more. I believe in loyalty and always have. And I think it is wonderful that you treat your vendors this way. And some day I hope to earn the same kind of loyalty from you. (Pacing and supporting.) Now as long as we are talking about loyalty, wouldn't you agree that loyalty to a vendor is great, but loyalty to your company is even greater? So, suppose we can demonstrate a method that would significantly upgrade the quality of your finished product and reduce your cost. Would you not agree that the greater loyalty to your company comes first?"

The beauty of mental judo is that it makes both parties feel like winners by preserving rapport in the relationship, by enhancing good feelings, and finally by redirecting the buyer to new and better options, all in an atmosphere devoid of hassle. The salesperson, therefore, is being truly of service and maintains control of the emotional climate.

WHEN TURNING TABLES IS APPRECIATED

The 400 sales and service representatives of the worldwide V Corporation have accounts whose annualized purchases range from a few thousand to a million dollars. When they make initial calls, some purchasing agents put them on notice that it might be years before they can expect an order. Industrial salespeople who want to build long-term relationships tend to avoid confrontations and sales brinkmanship. One purchasing agent is reported as saying, "Have patience. It could be three or four years. Your competitor had to wait that long to get his turn, but keep calling and keep us informed."

Here is how mental judo can save years. You say, "I have no problem with that. Thanks for letting me know what I can expect. That makes it a little bit easier and helps me budget my time. I appreciate it. Now let me do something for you in return. (Pacing and supporting.) Just suppose I can save $60,000 a year in one of your operations—and I have a specific one in mind—my question is, how long would you want to wait? A year would mean $60,000, two years $120,000, and three years $180,000. What do you think?"

The purchasing agent, now curious, asks for more details, until she has reason to believe that the sales representative's claim has merit. She arranges for a pilot test with her process engineering people, which is the first step to getting the order.

Once again, there are two winners; the customer and the sales representative. Both save money. Both save time. Both enhance their business relationship, all thanks to mental judo.

Unlike the Charlie story, where the sales representative focused away from formal education on to the even greater impact of sales attitudes, the salesperson here stays with the concept of patience but refocuses it to the cost of that patience as far as the customer is concerned.

TAKING THE BALL AWAY

In the management and sales seminar business, where corporate sales can easily exceed $100,000 per order, we occasionally hear, "Of course, you understand, we will also be getting in touch with one or two other companies in your field."

We respond by saying, "Thanks for letting us know. We encourage prospects to check with other companies, and we do ourselves when making major purchase decisions. If you want the most thorough possible information, while saving you time and money, I know of two major corporations of your size whose executives attended four or five showcase seminars by some of the best-known companies in our field. I will be pleased to give you their names as references. You can ask them what they discovered and why they decided on us."

In this true example, we agree with the need to investigate and check references, then refocus from having the prospect talk to one or two competitors to having him or her get reports on the five or six best known in the field. We are truly of service to our prospects by helping them increase their options.

A SLEIGHT OF MIND

Of the myriad of ways of dealing with objections, the mental judo technique using refocusing is the most agreeable and persuasive for both prospect and salesperson. It is a sleight of mind. Not only do you agree with the prospect completely, but you even reinforce him or her, making you seem totally nonthreatening. Now you use the very objection he or she is making and alert him or her to alternatives that make even better sense in his or her views. This literally enables you to refocus whatever your prospect is stuck on and redirect his or her priorities.

ETHICAL CONSIDERATIONS

Mental judo is a powerful technique. Its potency comes from the fact that it is both gentle and innovative. That, in fact, makes it one of the most awesome forms of hidden persuasion in action.

The use of mental judo is justified and ethical when the prospect truly needs a product or service and when the product or service is offered at a fair price. Many prospects cheat themselves out of opportunities to save or make money because of the games they play with salespeople. Mental judo cuts through gamesmanship by reeducating the prospect to greater options and better solutions.

It diminishes the chance of false issues clouding the prospect's perspective. The price objection, for example, is often a surface issue and an expression of laziness. Whether a product or service costs a few dollars more or less seldom tells you its cost in use. By the same token, not buying a needed product or service can make a difference to the detriment of the prospect.

When a company buys a new piece of equipment, it protects or increases its productivity edge over the competitor. When an investor purchases an underpriced stock, he or she takes advantage of an opportunity to make money. In instances such as these, a salesperson who does not use mental judo is derelict in his or her professional obligation. There are circumstances when it can actually be unethical and harmful to the prospect not to use this technique when it is called for. Mental judo is a force for positive good.

REFOCUSING YOUR LISTENER'S SENSE OF REALITY

Bob, the chairman of the board and an ex-congressman, was the subject of highly partisan newspaper articles, which labeled him high in integrity, outspoken, opinionated, ultra-conservative, and unbending. After attending our three-day management seminar, he invited me to address his management team for the purpose of voting yes or no to our services. There were 15 yes and one no. His was the no. Since he felt more equal than the others, he won. After lunch we returned to his office to review his decision. Here is how it went:

Me: "Bob, I want you to know I was pleased with your people's decision and disappointed at yours. I'd like you also to know that this does not affect our personal relationship in any way. I know you to be a man of integrity and personal courage, and I respect you for it."

Bob: "Thank you. I appreciate that. And I wouldn't have it any other way."

Me: "Bob, when you decided to cast your ballot against, you had your own good reasons for doing so. Now that that's behind us, would you mind sharing them with me?"

Bob: "Not at all. What would you like to know?"

Me: "What is the single most important reason, Bob, for voting no?"

Bob: "That's easy. We have a good group of managers here. They are capable and hard-working. There is no reason why we should need an outside consultant to turn things around. I can't remember when my father (founder of one of the state's largest corporations) ever used a consultant."

Me: "Bob, I was very impressed by the people I met this morning. It's easy for me to believe that they are professionals and that they do a good job. And I know you to be a person who doesn't do things without good reason. Let me ask you, what did you have in mind when you invited me here?"

Bob: "Well, I watched you in front of groups and I wanted you to address my people and put a little fire under them. Quite frankly, I was surprised at the way they voted."

Me: "Thanks for your candor, Bob. Frankly, I was a little surprised at their response myself. Now, here you are; you have excellent people and they're willing to work hard. My question to you is, why do you think they wanted to bring me in?"

Bob: "Because they are not making bonus. We aren't doing very well."

Me: "What will happen to them and the rest of this company if things continue the way they have been going?"

Bob: "Well, I'm afraid if we don't turn the boat around, and I mean soon, we might have to relocate down South."

Me: "When will that be?"

Bob: "Oh, in about nine months from now."

Me: "Bob, how long do you want to wait?"

Bob: (After a moment's silence.) "Get your appointment book out. When can you start?"

"What will happen if" is one of many refocusing techniques that can cause your listener to alter his or her perspective for reality. "What will happen if" specifically makes your listeners reflect on the consequences of their decisions. It gets them to focus more clearly on the future, on outcome. In an age of instant gratification, this has wide application.

Jack Nye had a chip on his shoulder. A good salesman, he was careful only to let his company's people see his critical attitude. Repeated confrontations with the sales manager brought no lasting change, so that the company seriously considered dismissing him. At their request, Jack and I spent some time together.

Me: "What will happen, Jack, if they tell you they have had enough and let you go?"

Jack: "I don't care. I'll get another sales job."

Me: "OK. What will happen then? Things won't probably be going as well as you expect there, either. So, sooner or later, you'll be driving them up a wall, too. Is that a good possibility?"

Jack: "It's a possibility."

Me: "And then what?"

Jack: "I'll get another sales job."

Me: "Right. About how old are you, Jack?"

Jack: "Thirty-seven. Why?"

Me: "Well, let's say it takes three years before you get yourself canned. How much longer do you expect to go through those cycles?"

Jack: (After a long silence.) "This may sound silly, but I never thought of it that way before. I better do something about it, or I won't ever get anywhere."

Me: "Right."

Jack has high standards, and when the company's internal support group fails him, he bares his teeth. Now that he is a little wiser, he treats the support people with the same persuasive skills he normally reserves for his customers. The reason for changing his behavior was the dour prospect of a lifetime of job-hopping, a refocus on his part.

Another refocusing technique is "Just suppose." It sounds particularly comfortable to your prospect's ears, because it feels so nonthreatening.

As previously mentioned, a giant corporation wanted its service personnel to do some selling when making service calls on businesses and residences. The people resisted, however, because they believed selling was hussling and hassling people. They also believed that their high technical competence would be besmirched by their lack of sales expertise and would color the customers' perception of them and their service. "Just suppose" to the rescue. After considerable training and coaching, they acquired the confidence to use it.

Martie Campbell was completing an installation.

> *Martie:* "Just suppose, Mr. Goodenough, you can have another unit anywhere in these offices. Where would you put it?"
>
> *Mr. Goodenough:* "You realize, young woman, that I'm not buying anything."
>
> *Martie:* "I understand, but just suppose you can have another unit anywhere on these premises. Where do you think you'd have it?"
>
> *Mr. Goodenough:* "Well, in that case, at the desk near the entrance."
>
> *Martie:* "Hm, interesting idea. Why there?"
>
> *Mr. Goodenough:* "Why? Because it is the most accessible spot, you don't have to interrupt anyone, and we probably would improve our service with it."
>
> *Martie:* "Good reasons. What model would you pick?"
>
> *Mr. Goodenough:* "What model? The off-white, medium size."
>
> *Martie:* "Why not the smaller one?"
>
> *Mr. Goodenough:* "Because it's too small for our workload."
>
> *Martie:* "Say, that's a good reason. Let me ask you, so long as that is the most accessible spot and you don't have to interrupt anyone, and at the same time you improve your operation and have the workload for it, why not save yourself some money and get it installed while I'm here? If you ordered it later and I had to come back to do it, there'd be another service charge. This way, you know you'll save $80."
>
> *Mr. Goodenough:* "That so? Hm. OK. Good idea. Let's do it."

The "Just suppose" is a multiservice tool. First, it seems so harmless that the prospect permits himself to discuss it. Second, the service person expands the prospect's thinking and makes him focus on positive reasons for owning the unit. Third, she gets the customer to come up with and voice the sales points himself, a sure convincer. Fourth, she uses an imbedded command when she states, "Just suppose, Mr. Goodenough, you can have another unit." Top sales producers do this unwittingly most of the time. Fifth, she hits home on saving $80 now, a minor decision point. Sixth, she discovers the prospect's buying fingerprints and seizes many opportunities for stroking his judgment.

On the lighter side, the "Just suppose" technique proved itself an effective opening ploy on the public dance floor of a nightclub, as one of our workshop participants demonstrated. A short, gray-haired man, he invited a taller and very attractive young woman to dance and was curtly rejected. He rejoined us at the table, had a few sips of wine, announced that he had a plan, and the next thing we knew they were dancing.

"How did you do that?" we asked.

"I used 'Just suppose.'"

"You did? How?"

"I went up to her and said, 'I know why you didn't want to dance with me. It is my size, right?' She said, 'Right.' So I said, 'I don't want to marry you. Just suppose I were six-foot-one and 34 years old. Would you dance with me?' 'Yes,' she smiled. She took me by the hand, and the next thing I knew we were dancing."

A final example of "Just suppose" has to do with choosing a new model car. My friend, a researcher by profession, visited a number of showrooms and discovered that in her price range the Japanese cars were the better buy. She had a model in mind. I suggested that she check accident reports in her area listing the cars involved and compare repair costs of American and Japanese models. To her surprise, American cars proved not only safer but also less expensive to repair. As a result of this refocus, she bought an American car.

There are a variety of techniques for refocusing other people's views of reality, including objections on price, delivery, quality, a prior bad experience, personality issues, and others. All of us have but five senses and filter what we take in through a welter of experiences and psychological biases. Often we are biased to a point where we hurt ourselves. Refocusing helps you expose your prospect to the significant factors he or she has failed to consider. Refocusing enables you to be of better service.

16

Big-Ticket
Corporate Selling

THE TWO MEANINGS OF BIG TICKET

Any transaction amounting to one digit trailed by a chain of six, seven, or eight zeroes qualifies as *big ticket*. Big ticket also describes the handful of corporate customers you find in nearly any industry, who with a few orders can account for a significant part of the annual consumption of your wares. Big ticket is used here as a counterweight to the hundreds of orders you would have to obtain to equal its weight in volume and profit. Big-ticket corporate selling introduces far more complexities to the sales process than ordinary, face-to-face encounters. Each corporation has its traditions and sacred cows, its unspoken rules, its culture and philosophy, its positive and negative triggers, and its politics. Just as each of us has a characteristic buying pattern—be it for a car, a video recorder, or a home—so does a company have its distinctive buying fingerprints. Just as you and I react to emotional words and ideas, so does a corporate prospect do the same.

To the novice, big-ticket corporate selling has the aspects of jungle uncertainty about it. What is there about the big-sale game hunters that is worth emulating? First, they know how to sniff out the unfamiliar territory that is the bailiwick of their new prospects and that they often do so before making their move. In the hallways of sales departments, military terms like G-2-ing (obtaining intelligence about) the prospect are familiar buzzwords.

Big-game sales hunters manage to identify and become personally acquainted with the real decision makers. They are alert to the positive influencers, the loyal opposition, the fence-sitters, and the pigeonholers. In this game it takes more than caring about people or persuasive skills. It takes the whole deck of maze brightness (informal intelligence) and influence management. It takes common sense, patience, resourcefulness, follow-through, and survival instinct. Big-ticket corporate selling is to ordinary sales what the space shuttle is to an ordinary plane. They both fly, but one is vastly more complex, vastly more difficult to get off the ground and land safely. Yet, once aloft, the space shuttle takes you farther, faster, and higher than any plane known. It is a headier experience.

THREE WAYS TO APPROACH THE CORPORATE PROSPECT

The processes of corporate communication and big-ticket corporate selling resemble each other. In corporate communication, 20 percent of the essence of a message is lost between each echelon. Bottom-up does not survive through the layers because of reinterpretation and hidden agendas. Lateral has the advantage of excellent communication among peers, only 5 percent getting lost between one person and other, but suffers because there still has to be a top-down and bottom-up to spread through the whole organization.

In big-ticket corporate selling, top-down is fastest but may lose effectiveness as it filters through the management layers. The sales professional takes nothing for granted, as he or she shepherds the product or service through the echelons. Lateral is slower and requires even more effort to percolate down to subordinates and up to the top executives. Bottom-up rarely overcomes the natural pull of gravity, and like corporate communication it does not reach the top, but there have been important exceptions. What this is saying is that selling to large corporations of itself is not difficult, but qualifying for the big-ticket label is.

Each approach has advantages to customer and sales representative alike. Each is a function of the customer's budget and influence. For example, the corporate staffer may reject your service, but the divisions having the wherewithal may welcome you with open arms. Usually there is a best way, and often it is the only way. When selling large-scale consulting services, such as reviewing the organizational structure or identifying significant profit leaks, the wisest approach is through the executive suite only. Without the wholehearted interest and consent from that office, there can be no sale. And for good reason. Who can authorize the large-scale fee, and who has authority to mandate this kind of undertaking but the chief executive?

Top-down is also employed when companywide surveys and analyses can uncover potentially large savings in time and material. This approach may appeal to control-minded top management, receive only lukewarm acceptance from executives interested in participative management, and actually generate overt resistance from machine operators and clerks, who know the most about their job but were not consulted. Strategists working for big-ticket sales know the difference between making a sale and having a customer. The sale is only the entrance ticket. Now the real work can begin.

The lateral route leads through the division manager or the department manager, such as the vice-president of human resources or the telecommunication manager. Even when they buy your proposition, they still have to sell it upstairs, which means that to gain acceptance they have to go on the mat for you. Their reputation is on the line, and they will be identified with the success of the venture. Usually they call meetings to have others join in alliance with them so that their compatriots are in the boat. This takes time. Often they are more receptive to a trial run, a pilot, or whatever constitutes a sampling before lending their full endorsement. Sales professionals offer their special skills and abilities in selling and servicing the product or service to others in the company. This is why the lateral approach takes more time and why the dollar amounts are smaller in the beginning. In very formal companies, niching yourself at the middle management level may make your job of reaching top management all the harder. Once you go over their heads without their consent, you lose their loyalty. The result of the lateral strategy may mean doing some business in one part of the company, while other parts may stay closed to you for political reasons. Lateral niching is a more difficult road to big-ticket selling, simply because more hurdles have to be overcome.

The bottom-up strategy usually starts with an ordinary sale at a low level in the decision-making process, which may eventually blossom into a big-ticket sale as a result of your excellent product, service, and situational sensitivity. Years may go by as you grow with the customer. In the manufacturing industry, to name one, this grass-roots approach has historically been the favored route to what may culminate in big-ticket selling. By building on years of friendship and loyalty with the men and women in the plant, your competitor will have great difficulty in replacing you over the long haul. The quality circle concept, when properly followed and administered, favors the bottom-up strategy.

REAL PROBLEMS AND BUGABOOS

An old sales adage holds that easy-to-see people have all kinds of time and no money, and hard-to-see people have all kinds of money and no time. The CEO is hard to reach and even harder to meet. But once he or she gives you your chance, things begin to move. Available statistics show that you save months, sometimes years, when you present your product or service and yourself properly to the chief. This presents no special difficulty when you have many things in common, such as age, education, experience, sex, and social background. But what if there is a generation gap or any number of other real or imagined barriers? What if you are a 25-year-old woman making $35,000 calling on a CEO twice your age and earning ten times your income? What do you two have in common except your differences? What do you talk about? What does this do to your self-confidence?

Do what any top producer would do. Do your homework by having your center of influence pave the way to introduce you in glowing terms. Let him or her make the appointment and presell you. Get all of the vital statistics about your prospect—age, family, children, education, career path, special areas of interest, hobbies, sports, travel, and church. The more you know, the fewer will be the surprises, the less likely the missteps, and the greater the feeling of quiet self-confidence. When you have no true center of influence, get as much information as possible from the person who gave you the lead. If you lack the necessary referral, try the self-generating referral system described in Chapter 11. What if your target account is thousands of miles away, perhaps in Europe or Asia? Again, emulate the top producers by doing your research. Dun and Bradstreet and others can provide you with reasonably up-to-date information about corporations and their officers in this country. Various consultants and government and private agencies can furnish information about foreign companies and governments. Nothing beats preparation, even when you are told to make a cold telephone call on a major prospect right now. At the very least, prepare yourself for a variety of evasions, stalls, and objections by developing some mental judo and refocusing techniques described in Chapter 15. It will do wonders for your self-image.

WHEN FACE TO FACE WITH THE CEO

The easiest way to overcome fear of another person is to decide to like him or her. Your eyes and voice signal the feeling without extra help from you. Have something in your head or hand to start the interview. By pacing speech, mood, and body language, you automatically find yourself concentrating on the prospect and away from yourself. Respond in their preferred language by tracking eye movements. When he or she looks up right, then down right, for example, say, "As you can imagine..." and "You will soon feel the impact of..." This promotes trust and rapport without the prospect's conscious awareness. Trust can be further enhanced with some self-disclosure statements (pacing what is undeniably true) and getting permission to ask some pertinent questions as described in Chapter 7 and Chapter 8. The CEO may decide to introduce you to others in the company or continue to work with you. In any event, you are making good progress, because you are an intelligent listener, a keen observer, and an on-target responder. The prospect will come to accept and respect you and become your ally no matter what your age or sex. As a show of good manners on your part, you drop him or her a personal note of thanks without making a sales letter out of it.

THE TOP-DOWN STRATEGY

Just as a big-game hunter takes a native guide, a big-ticket corporate sales master finds an advocate. For whatever reason, a company may have its unfriendly natives and quicksands past which you must pick your way. Power, influence, and politics shift like sand as corporate officers and managers are moved to new responsibilities.

The chief executive officer is your best advocate. When you succeed in making a presentation and he or she in turn introduces you to the subordinates, your chances of selling them are good. Even if he or she only agrees to shake your hand and refers you to other managers, you at least come in under his or her aegis. Violate this principle, and it will take months, often years, longer to accomplish the same result.

Your next best guide is a center of influence, a person either in or outside the company who has over time developed a lot of influence with the decision maker. Usually an insider, an officer, or a manager can be especially valuable to you.

How can you arrange to meet the decision makers and the centers of influence you do not yet know? You do so by having customers in similar positions refer you to them. You can also create your own internal referrals, as described in Chapter 11.

CREATING YOUR OWN REFERRALS

In many companies, corporate officers other than the CEO may be receptive to your story and then give you direction on how to proceed. If they are impressed by what they hear, they may act as a conduit for you.

I was marketing a service to a multinational company, a builder of transportation equipment and vehicles, but had no referral to them. As is my custom, I decided to see the highest-placed corporate officer who would receive me and was encouraged to be granted an audience. The man listened to my story, then told me exactly how to proceed and allowed me to use him as a referral. I followed through and got to see the decision maker, a vice-president/general manager. Success? Far from it. After I met with him a couple of times, the vice-president/ general manager referred me to peer and subordinate managers, each on a one-to-one basis. I realized I was running an obstacle course with no guarantee for success. Fortunately, I was permitted to check the vice-president/general manager's sales temperature from time to time to be sure of his continued support. We also agreed that I could voice concern about possible negative encounters with others. It was all right to relay to him any delaying tactics or evidence of resistance, so that he could prepare his own brand of gentle suasion. Clearing hurdle after hurdle and with success at last in sight, I ran smack into a wall in the person of the vice-president of personnel.

The meeting was a disaster from the start. The man had his own agenda and was blasé. I reported my apprehension to my contact and asked for help. I got it. A short time later everyone was in the boat, and the company placed the order.

I succeeded for several reasons, but survived because of three: First, I made sure that the vice-president/general manager himself was sold. Second, I followed through on the decision-making pattern he had established. Third, I reported on the outcome of each questionable interview. Because I built a communication lifeline, the vice-president/general manager was able to obtain a consensus. A friendly insider can help you to avoid mistakes. An advocate can steer you through the maze.

SELLING TO A COMMITTEE

Initially, it is important to distinguish between an in-company group and a public group, especially as concerns presentation and strategy. Every corporate leader, every union leader, has experienced time and again that a group does not behave like the sum of its parts. Especially in today's atmosphere of participative management, a president may readily defer to a subordinate when it comes to a final decision. That alone emphasizes that no one on a committee can be discounted or ignored. In addition, each committee has a personality all its own, which can either work for you or against you. Somehow, someone will assume the role of devil's advocate or district attorney while your presentation is in progress. Since this is a statistical likelihood, you should be prepared to disarm the objection by raising and answering it before it comes up. Your listeners will be favorably impressed with your balanced approach and fair-mindedness.

You will cover all information bases by talking in auditory, visual, and kinesthetic terms. Every listener will be riveted by your language and absorbed by your descriptions.

There are two reasons for this. When you express yourself in the listeners' favorite sensory language, they find it easy to listen. When you speak in another sensory language, it is harder and requires them to concentrate more. Use all three information channels—auditory, visual, kinesthetic—when talking to a group, and you can cover all bases.

Some of the great presenters make a point of having eye contact with everyone in the audience, if only for a moment. They do this to acknowledge each and every person individually. They will also personally shake everyone's hand, if possible, to reinforce the bond. By following their example and using auditory, visual, and kinesthetic languages, you succeed in establishing a strong tie between the individuals of your audience and yourself.

Where time and geography permit, we suggest getting a couple of committee members in your corner before presentation day. Your best choice usually is to make a dress rehearsal presentation to the decision maker alone. By reviewing your speech and passing on it, he or she in effect becomes your ally.

Best of all, this strategy of individual meetings with each committee member, though time-consuming, almost always assures the best end results. First, you establish trust and rapport; second, you learn of his or her concerns and special insights; and, third, each member has become acquainted with your presentation, enabling each to understand the critical points.

RSVP TO MY RFP

The Sale Begins When the Customer Says No is the title of an old book on salesmanship. From personal observation in working with others and being involved four-square in big-ticket corporate selling, I would retitle the situation today *The Sale Begins When the Customer Hesitates and Stalls.* Many of the businesspeople you and I encounter are so concerned with confrontations that they do not give themselves permission to be reasonably straightforward and plain-spoken. What has that to do with a request for proposal (RFP)? Many salespeople, even experienced ones, trap themselves into believing that an RFP is tantamount to an expression of serious interest. In too many instances it is not. It is the same as "Send me a brochure."

What can you do to avoid the wasted time and effort in writing proposals? And what can you do to sell what is in your proposal? Do you judge the prospect's request as an expression of serious interest or a way of terminating the interview? If you are unsure, get permission to ask questions regarding specifics. Who besides this person are the other decision makers? When can they be convened to be present at your proposal presentation? What kind of people are they? Would it not be a good idea to receive their input first? When are they going to want delivery, assuming everything is on target? What would have to happen to make your listeners feel good about the proposal? What would they be seeing and hearing? Should you send the proposal in the mail? Our experience indicates that it generates a lot of questions, which allow us to customize our product or service to their needs.

Some of our large subcontractor clients seemed to invest more time in proposal writing than in any other business activity. We counted the ratio of proposals to contracts, raised the bar of conditions higher, and improved the contract awarded ratio from 1 in 11 to 1 in 3. This ratio showed us to be too selective, because we filtered out too many borderline cases. As a result we lowered the bar to a 1 in 4 ratio and experienced a jolting spurt foward in business revenues.

Some of my biggest sales were closed on a handshake with the CEO and did not depend on a formal proposal initially. Subsequently, we would prepare one as a method of confirmation. Suppose your industry custom is RFP? How do you handle the situation? Where possible, be the last to submit your proposal, and do so in person. Go over each major point and sell. Ask permission to ask questions, so that you can tailor the design to the prospect as much as possible. When you run into serious difficulty and feel you may not get the contract, suggest small tests, feasibility studies, or a pilot installation, so that you can learn more how to be of excellent service to that prospect now and later.

Establish and cement relationships with the decision makers and influencers. Let them get to know you and your professional dedication. Earn their trust and respect, check on the accuracy of your perception of their behavior style and information bias, and pace speech, body language, and the future. A top salesperson is a problem solver, a feature translator, and a creator of the proper emotional climate. Follow in these footsteps, and you will exceed your reasonable expectations.

INDEX